INSPIRED TO GREATNESS

A FEMININE APPROACH TO HEALING THE WORLD

TRACY ULOMA COOPER

Chiron Publications
Asheville, North Carolina

www.ChironPublications.com

Cover and interior image by Getty Image
Interior and cover design by Lisa Alford
Printed primarily in the United States of America.

ISBN 978-1-63051-404-4 paperback
ISBN 978-1-63051-405-1 hardcover
ISBN 978-1-63051-406-8 electronic

Library of Congress Cataloging-in-Publication Data Names:
Cooper, Tracy Uloma, author.
Title: Inspired to greatness : a feminine approach to healing
the world / by Tracy Uloma Cooper.
Description: Asheville, North Carolina : Chiron
Publications, [2016] |
Includes bibliographical references and index.
Identifiers: LCCN 2016044602 (print) | LCCN 2016058065
(ebook) | ISBN 9781630514044 (pbk. : alk. paper) | ISBN
9781630514051 (hardcover : alk. paper) | ISBN
9781630514068 (E-book)
Subjects: LCSH: Self-realization in women. | Self-esteem in
women. |Leadership in women.
Classification: LCC HQ1206 .C72125 2016 (print) | LCC
HQ1206 (ebook) | DDC 305.4--dc23
LC record available at https://lccn.loc.gov/2016044602

BOOK DEDICATION AND ACKNOWLEDGMENTS

The book *Inspired to Greatness: A Feminine Approach to Healing the World* was a process of intense internal growth and is graciously dedicated to the generous individuals who have been soul guides positively impacting my entire life. I lovingly acknowledge hero and role model my mother Susan and grandmother Marion for their unconditional love, support, and faith; my therapist Shirley McNeal, the navigator who assisted to chart a path towards my most authentic self; my first professional mentor and friend Kathy Wagner Sacks, who took me under her wing; excellent professors who impacted my intellectual development at the universities I attended; the participants who trusted me with the intimate details of their successes and frailties; Chiron Publications and Jennifer Fitzgerald, for your professionalism at each point in the publishing process; Antonio Herreria Fernandez, who sat with me editing each line; the numerous other mentors who touched my life; and myself for the courage to engage in this journey and believe in myself!

TABLE OF CONTENTS

QUIZ

Welcome to *Inspired to Greatness: A Feminine Approach to Healing the World*. As we begin this journey together, we invite you to take a separate piece of paper and immerse yourself in the following quiz. This is your time for non-judgmental self-reflection and unabashed authenticity, take a moment just for YOU. Your self-evaluation offers personal insight into your current state of Empowerment, Balance and Happiness. You will find the answers to your questions throughout the pages of this book. Once you have reached the book's conclusion, please review your responses to assess your level of empowerment. Onwards & upwards…

1. Do you feel empowered?

If you answered "Yes" to #1

a. As an empowered woman, what character traits do you believe are significant in the lives of you and other empowered women?

b. What life-enhancing strategies did you employ that led to your feeling of empowerment?

c. What life experiences, critical moments, and influential individuals do you feel were significant or formative in developing your present sense of empowerment?

If you answered "No" to #1

a. Do you know women who are empowered?

→ Yes

  i. What traits do they exhibit that demonstrate they are empowered women?

  ii. How would you describe the empowered woman's life?

→ No

  i. What traits do you think an empowered woman encompasses?

  ii. If you were to imagine an empowered woman, how would you describe her life?

b. What would make you feel more empowered?

If you answered "Conditional/Maybe" to #1

a. Would you describe the times/situations you feel empowered? How do you feel? What is occurring?

b. Would you describe the times/situations you do not feel empowered? How do you feel? What is occurring?

c. What would make you feel empowered more often?

2. On a scale of 1-10, how empowered do you feel?

HAPPY SECTION

1. On a scale of 1-10, how happy are you?
2. Do you like the way you live your life?
3. Is your life supporting you and whom you really are?
4. At what point were you the most happy in your life?
5. What made this the happiest time of your life?
6. In making decisions, do you ever ask yourself which option would bring you the most happiness?
7. (Mythologist Joseph Campbell spoke of following your true passion and finding your bliss.) In an ideal world, if money, responsibility, and other people's opinions were not an issue, what would make you happy for the rest of your life?
8. Why are you not doing this today?
9. What can you do today to increase your level of happiness?

BALANCE SECTION

1. How often do you feel stressed? (Frequently, Sometimes, Rarely, Never)
2. What are some of the ways you overfunction or feel overburdened in your daily life?
3. What are you tolerating that is not good for you or that you do not like or do not want?
4. How often do you say no?
5. Do you feel cherished and appreciated?
6. On most days, do you feel feminine, soft, and vulnerable or masculine, hard, and action orientated?
7. Please list positive qualities of being a woman and positive qualities of being a man, if combined could benefit society. Explain why.

WRAP-UP SECTION

1. Time magazine conducted a poll, and the results stated that women are more educated, more powerful than ever before, but are less happy. Why do you feel the women polled felt this way?
2. In the Time magazine poll, women rated various words in order of importance for themselves and the results were as follows: (1) Interesting

Career, (2) Financial Success, (3) Happy Marriage and Children. When the same women were asked what they would want most for their own daughters, they ranked in order of importance the exact opposite: (1) Happy Marriage and Children, (2) Financial Success, and (3) Interesting Career. Why do you think the women polled wanted something different for themselves than they wanted for their own daughters? (Why did the women polled want something different for their daughters?)

3. Is there anything else we haven't discussed in our time together that you would like to share about your empowerment and happiness?

NOTES

CHAPTER 1
INTRODUCTION

GLOBAL POSITIONING SERVICE

My own journey toward empowerment inspired my research on women's empowerment. This personal journey in turn has deepened my intention to touch and be of service to the collective. I am inspired to witness other women's stories and to explore what it means to women to feel happy and empowered as a woman. It is my intention to elucidate and demonstrate the gift of women's personal experience of empowerment and self-reported happiness through documenting and analyzing their stories.

My path toward self-empowerment and happiness was one of integration, encompassing a willingness to delve into my unconscious. The process involved surrendering to the material encountered in the unconscious, making a conscious effort to remain open, while undergoing emotional catharsis, and emerging more balanced increasingly able to trust in something greater than myself.

As a young woman, I followed the establishment of social norms and behaved the way others expected me to behave, thus creating a false persona. Jung (1921/1971) describes the persona as "a functional complex that comes into existence for reasons of adaptation or personal convenience, but is by no means identical with the individuality" (p. 465). My persona had a tendency to take on more than I wanted – I was responsible to a fault, held unreasonable expectations and standards for myself, and would not ask for help. Personas are "only a mask of the collective psyche, a mask that feigns individuality," Jung explains (1928/1972, p. 157). Yet, over time, my defenses and coping strategies deteriorated in the attempt to sustain a false mask. The state of inauthenticity led to irritation, stress, anxiety, fear, and a feeling of being overwhelmed. Ultimately, fearing "something may easily happen that will bring into consciousness an unwelcome portion of their real individual character" (1928/1972, p. 157), I repressed my emotions, and sensitivities welled up like a dormant volcano heading to eruption. I feared, however, that if I surrendered to the eruption, a lifetime's worth of unfinished torments trying to find a release would destroy me.

As part of my psychology program, one of the requirements was to engage in therapy as a means to access our inner feelings and to be able to connect with patients in the future. Therapy enabled me to realize it had taken a lot of energy to maintain control of the façade and that I longed to liberate my internal tenderness.

I learned that "the aim of individuation is nothing less than to divest the self of the false wrappings of the persona" (Jung, 1959/1980, p. 174). Gradually, I moved toward finding safe outlets for my feelings, rather than holding them in and containing them. Through acknowledging my feelings and embracing intuition as "affectively-charged judgments that arise through rapid, non-conscious, and holistic associations" (Hodgkinson, 2008, p. 4), I immersed myself in the emotional depths of the deep sea within me. Thus, it was through developing this connection with myself that lead to feelings of unconditional acceptance and trust in my ability to remain true to my needs, in any given moment.

A goal of my pilgrimage was to accept my flawed self. I learned that mistakes made me human, and that I could grow from them and move toward grounded humility. In *The Spirituality of Imperfection*, Kurtz and Ketcham (1993) suggest that spirituality begins with the acceptance of our innate imperfection as human beings and that blame toward ourselves or others is unnecessary. I am still learning not to push myself past the breaking point, being compassionate towards myself, and accepting the importance of good self-care. I have begun to transition from doing to being.

Gaining self-empowerment was a karmic crossroads marked by a challenging testing period that led me to greater maturity. Profound and critical moments allowed me to be able to integrate suffering into a deeper faith. This was an epic test of claiming more internal power to be able to feel stronger and more integrated. From a Jungian perspective, the acceptance, integration, and wholeness derived from expressing any number of qualities, ranging in the continuum from masculine to feminine energies, are key components.

> Unfortunately our Western mind, lacking all culture in this respect, has never yet devised a concept, nor even a name, for the union of opposites through the middle path, that most fundamental item of inward experience, which could be set against the Chinese concept of Tao. It is at once the most individual fact and the most universal, the most legitimate fulfillment of the meaning of the individual's life. (Jung, 1953/1977, p. 205)

Inner strength was gained through bringing to consciousness the hitherto masculine aspects of my personality in terms of setting boundaries with loved ones and learning the importance of limit setting. While setting those boundaries, I incorporated the aspects of my feminine by asking for and accepting help and self-nurturance. Internal balance was integral to my evolution. A key landmark in my voyage toward empowerment was becoming a collaborator with my inner strength to determine when to apply the right amount of gentle strength and gauging when resting and self-care was more appropriate. This process of acceptance enabled me to access unconscious drives, thereby freeing up energy to feel at home within myself.

In Jung's theories, mental and emotional disturbances are an attempt to find personal and spiritual wholeness (1943/1972, p. 110). Ultimately, the therapeutic work helped me to be more authentic, balanced, whole, and happy, and to gain the courage to cherish and show my true nature as a woman.

Foundationally, the origin of my interest and transference to the topic stems from women historically and the women in my family as part of revealing dynamics involving their struggle towards empowerment and happiness. Attending to the stories of women in my motherline led me to wonder, what factors contribute to a woman's empowerment? Does an empowered woman feel happier through the beneficial qualities emerging from balancing the masculine and feminine within her?

My grandmother held great potential for the expression of empowerment; however, she chose to repress her personal needs due to societal expectations. She made my grandfather's health her focus, her family's needs a second priority, and her own happiness an afterthought. Her subjugation was due to the repression of self strongly tied to the dominant view of women's roles in society in her time. In *Time* magazine's the "State of the American Woman" article the "New Woman in 1972," stay-at-home mother Lauretta Galligan echoes my grandmother's perspective: "My first priority is my family and my husband's work" (p. 29). In a 2009 follow-up report, Lauretta Galligan said, "It used to be that a man would be ashamed to be found in the kitchen.... Those old stereotypes have been buried forever. I think it's good that we got rid of most of them. I can't think of any that we'd want to hold on to" (Fitzpatrick, 2009, p. 29).

My mother, a member of the baby boomer generation, witnessed my grandmother and the women of the era's suppression of personal needs, struggled with uncertainty of appropriate expression of self and journeyed through extremes attempting to feel empowered and find happiness. In their youth, some women of the baby boomer generation still learned that a woman's role was to be obedient and place others first, but as they became adults, benefitting from women's liberation, many women found the freedom to acknowledge their own needs, to be independent, and to assert their will (Evans & Avis, 1999). My mother, as well as other women of her generation, struggled with the guilt and paradox of 1950s traditional role models while attempting to identify and project an image of the 1970s feminist model, the latter through the demonstration of how an empowered woman should represent herself to society. "It is not easy to be simultaneously the earth mother-goddess and the hard-bitten, hard-nosed corporate executive or fire person" (p. 190). This paradox led to an identity crisis for many men and women, who concurrently have to come to terms with shifting conventional roles in relationships. For example, considered a controversial, aggressive public woman throughout her political career, Hillary Rodham Clinton, a member of the baby boomer generation, states,

> I have often thought of myself and my friends as transitional figures, more sure of where we were coming from than where we were going. Friends of mine have

described our coming of age as being on the cusp of changes that fundamentally redefined the role of women. (Evans & Avis, 1999, p. xiii)

Those within the Baby Boomer generation are exploring the alternatives to women playing a passive, submissive role often reverting with aggressiveness to match that of their male counterparts, which seemed the only option available to women in such situations. Today, women of the baby boomer generation are experimenting with balance. All women need to find a balance that works for them in any specific situation, whether work requires more attention to competent independent skills or home necessitates a more feminine role (Evans & Avis, 1999). Rather than becoming attached to one role, the challenge is to find a balance and move between each as feels comfortable to the individual.

Currently, I, my sisters, friends, and other women of our generation have unlimited personal and professional possibilities open to us due to the efforts of our mothers and past generations. Yet, the recession has affected generations of women by placing many of us in the role of primary breadwinners (and heads) of household, as our significant others have been laid off or their income has declined or the marriage felt the impacts of divorce. In general, typical male dominated positions in white collar, middle management have been downsized while female dominated positions such as nursing, marketing, and account management have remained intact. Traditional roles have changed in this current economic climate, and this has implications for society. This amplifies the relevance of *Time* magazine's the "State of the American Woman," where "as women have gained more freedom, more education, and more economic power, they have become less happy" (Gibbs, 2009, p. 29). This article highlights the question can a woman be empowered and be happy? Can embracing the paradox of opposites and balancing the opposing forces of masculine and feminine aspects in both men and women's personalities help to achieve the goal of individual happiness, and the overarching goal of benefitting our society as a whole?

My predisposition to this topic and personal goal is a balanced self-empowerment, recognizing myself as both fire and damsel, integrating the male and female energies to create a powerful and beautiful human being. Intuitively, my discernment dictates that in the middle lies a path that will serve my greatest good. Within me falls the history of my family and the generations of women before me. I understand that I must explore the edges of light and dark, passivity and aggression, in order to feel the tension between the opposites. This journey involves being conscious of removing the mask of controlled perfection and authentically knowing and expressing myself through waking up to being who I am, standing up for, believing in, and loving who I am. The key to attain this goal is to trust, accept, share, and value my own rich emotional depths; my desire for passionate interchange expressing my powerful emotional needs so that others can help me meet and respond to those needs. This process will continue until a crumbling of the old structures falls and an internal disarmament occurs, becoming the laughing Buddha, the joyful peaceful center. This is where the true internal image of an empowered woman lies.

FOCUS, PLEASE

The aim of this book is to ascertain the factors that contribute to a woman's empowerment and to explore whether this correlates to her overall degree of happiness. The research involves the analysis of narratives derived from one-on-one interviews. The analysis results in a description of the themes and patterns found in the interviews.

The New Webster's Dictionary defines *empowerment* as to "empower, v. to give power" (Webster, 1986, p. 59). In Louise Hay's "Empowering Women" she refers to empowerment as "helping women reach their true potential" (1997, p. xi). This suggests that the factors that contribute to empowering women are the major influences and experiences that assist in giving women power and reaching their true potential. Influenced by Carl Jung's *anima* and *animus* concepts, this book hypothesized that harmonizing the full spectrum of masculine and feminine traits within an individual is an important factor that contributes to empowerment and increases happiness for men and women.

> According to Buddhism for a man to be perfect there are two qualities that he should develop equally: compassion (feminine) on one side, and wisdom (masculine) on the other. Here compassion represents love, charity, kindness, tolerance and such noble qualities on the emotional side,

or qualities of the heart, while wisdom would stand for the intellectual side or the qualities of the mind. If one develops only the emotional neglecting the intellectual, one may become a good-hearted fool: while to develop only the intellectual side neglecting the emotional may turn one into a hard-hearted intellect without feeling for others. Therefore, to be perfect one has to develop both equally. (Rahula, 1959, p. 46)

The aforementioned Buddhist philosophical approach has conceptual similarities to Jung's ideology, where men and women share feminine and masculine attributes. Jung describes his concepts as "the conscious principle (discrimination and cognition) in man (the paternal) Logos, and the principle of relatedness (connective quality) in women (the maternal) Eros. The inferior Eros in man I designate as anima and the inferior Logos in woman as animus" (Jung, 1982, p. 136). Jung believed that women's feminine egos are compensated by an unconscious masculine archetype and men's conscious masculine egos are compensated by an unconscious feminine archetype. The role of these archetypes, the anima or animus, is to lend assistance and complement the primary conscious personality in the foreground. As such, Jung delineates the difference between animus and anima:

> The anima produces *moods*, so the animus produces opinions; and as the moods of a man issue from a shadowy background, so the opinions of a woman rest on equally unconscious prior assumptions. Animus opinions very often have the character of solid convictions that are not likely shaken, or of principles whose validity is seemingly unassailable. (Jung, 1982, pp. 95–96)

In essence, the psyche's subpersonalities begin underdeveloped and primitive and have the ability to produce feelings and attitudes in opposition to the personality in the foreground.

By plumbing the depths of their unconscious, individuals are given the capacity to distinguish helpful from disruptive attributes and select advantageous traits to meld together to create a balanced personality. In terms of the animus, Jung references "its 'discriminative function,' which 'gives to women's consciousness a capacity for reflection, deliberation, and self-knowledge,' and its qualities of creativity, procreativity, assertiveness, and initiative" (1982, p. 179). Case in point, a woman's relationship with her inner masculine enhances the manner in which she approaches life. The animus provides her the wisdom to determine what she needs and how to acquire it (Jung, 1982). The feminine insight gained through the anima for a man grants relationship and relatedness, enabling him to bring forth his work and express his entire personality without suppressing any constructive aspects. As such, the benefits of the animus and anima are worthy of further exploration for both the individual and society.

> The Sacred Masculine is whole and wholly itself only when it is fused at the greatest possible depth and intensity with the Sacred Feminine. In so fusing with its "opposite," the "masculine" would transform its tendency to alienation, half-psychotic detachment, and the pursuit of power at the expense of life, into a strong, majestic, and undauntable power of loving and brave action within the world and within society to transform them both...while masculine, allowing the fullness and glory of the feminine to inform, inspire, and complete him. (Harvey, 1998, p. 150)

The unification of the Sacred Masculine and the Sacred Feminine brings healing to the current psyche split within women and men, leading to tolerance and compassion within humanity.

Jung summarizes, "She longs for greater consciousness, which would enable her to name her goals and give it meaning, and thus escape the blind dynamism of nature.... The woman of today is faced with a tremendous cultural task – perhaps it will be the dawn of a new era" (1982, p. 75).

Having in mind Jung's approach, we can state that reconciling the male and female aspects within individual women produces internal balance and feelings of wholeness. The analysis of the interviews, as we will demonstrate in the following chapters, determines each woman's current state of balance between her masculine and feminine energies and how it correlates to her levels of empowerment and happiness. In this sense, individual women may fall on various parts of the spectrum. We may classify these women into three different categories: the women who balance their masculine and feminine energies, women who consciously need to integrate their animus to derive benefits from masculine qualities, and, finally, women whose animus unconsciously drives their lives requiring them to recover a relation to the feminine. Thus, this book explores through interviews women's own ideas about their empowerment and happiness and whether they believe the integration of masculine and feminine energies is a relevant component; an important aspect that differentiates this book.

HAPPY EMPOWERED WOMEN

Empowering women is the best thing we can do for the planet. When women are suppressed, everybody loses. When women win, we all win (Hay, 1997, p. xi).

In *Bluebird, Women and the New Psychology of Happiness*, author Ariel Gore asked the question "can a woman be smart, empowered, and happy?" (Gore, 2010, p. appendix) This is, indeed, the question at the heart of this book.

May we, by analyzing empowerment and happiness, determine practical methods that women can implement to benefit society as a whole in the 21st century? Indeed, this feat is accomplished through the insights gleaned from the women's responses that identifies factors that may benefit other women.

This book and the analysis of the participants' subjective story telling will enable and help society to model effective interventions, treatments, and modalities designed specifically to address women's growing roles in the new realities of today's world while balancing their inherent need to be happy in a compassionate manner.

Defining the factors which contributes to women's empowerment while exploring its correlations to her overall degree of happiness is a critical contribution to society. Supporting this theory, the poll in Time magazine's Special Report, "The State of the American Woman," concludes that, "as women have gained more freedom, more education, and more economic power, they have become less happy" (Gibbs, 2009, p. 29). The survey suggests the need for research on women's empowerment bringing forward the importance of distributing information in a manner a nonprofessional may comprehend, duplicate, and use as an effective tool.

In response to the evolution beyond traditional female roles, women are experiencing pressure and confusion, as many find themselves transitioning from being the subaltern, within the classical household role, to a single parent who becomes the head of household with the financial responsibilities attached to it but without the support.

In relation to the previous statement, the Time/Rockefeller Foundation poll reveals that women have indeed become a dominant force in recent years, earning 57% of college degrees and making 75% of buying decisions at home (Gibbs, 2009). However, as noted above, some research indicates that women's level of happiness has declined in relation to their growth in status. Nevertheless, we can identify influences proving a woman has the capacity to be empowered in a manner that benefits both her community and herself.

Numerous studies have submerged themselves into women's issues in relation to empowerment, yet, in many cases, they approach the matter through a partial lens. This leaves them unable to grasp the overall problem and its solutions. In addition to this problematic, many also fail to impact society by not reaching the wider public, even though there are now so many highly accessible ways of communicating our results.

By integrating empowerment, Jung's animus and anima theory and psychological happiness and how this relates to actual lived contemporary female experience displayed in the interviews conducted, we can identify models of effective interventions, treatments, and modalities designed specifically to balance women's growing roles in society with their need to be happy. The interviews and their analysis will enrich the information available to women through hearing other women speak their own truths, having their own voice, concerning what contributes to their empowerment and happiness.

One example of today's shift in collective values occurring worldwide may be exemplified in *New York Times Magazine's* "Saving the World's Women – The Women's Crusade," where Nicholas D. Kristof and Sheryl WuDunn state:

> "Women hold up half the sky," in the words of a Chinese saying, yet that's mostly an aspiration: in a large slice of the world, girls are uneducated and women marginalized, and it's not an accident that those same

countries are disproportionately mired in poverty and riven by fundamentalism and chaos. There's a growing recognition among everyone from the World Bank to the U.S. military's Joint Chiefs of Staff to organizations like CARE that focusing on women and girls is the most effective way to fight global poverty and extremism. That's why foreign aid is increasingly directed to women. The world is awakening to a powerful truth: Women and girls aren't the problem; they're the solution. (2009)

Women are the solution. We conclude society has a moral obligation to support women's growing roles as an effective strategy to benefit the collective.

RESEARCH, RESEARCH, RESEARCH

Only when our entire culture for the first time saw itself threatened by radical doubt and critique did hermeneutics become a matter of universal significance. (Gadamer, 1960/1988, p. 100)

We approach women's empowerment from a phenomenological hermeneutic perspective utilizing the method of narrative analysis. The insight established from the "lived experiences" of the women are interpreted, and then condensed into themes related to women's empowerment and its correlation to happiness.

It is important to take note, that although the hermeneutic insight established from the interviews may have some degree of subjectivity, we may identify and define common patterns. Nevertheless, it is important before conducting any study to be mindful of whether the participant's self-reports represent a true reflection of an objective definition of empowerment. This is due to the historical subalternity of women within society and their fear of speaking for themselves. Thus, the participants interviewed may fall anywhere on the spectrum from being empowered to a lack of empowerment. With this insight, we have taken into account the potentiality of the individuals involved in the study may project an image of themselves as they would like to be seen. This aspect relates to personality and identity. In this sense, the formation of each identity may transition over the lifespan of an individual, not only developing during childhood. The process of identity involves moving through differentiation and individualization.

A portion of this transformation period is spent struggling with other individuals for the need to be right as they determine their belief structures, mature, and consolidate an identity. A part of identity is the concept of differentiation, which may be defined as "living according to your own values and beliefs in the face of opposition... while also having the ability to change your values, beliefs, and behavior when your well-considered judgment or concern for others dictates it" (Schnarch, 1997, pp. 47-48). During this time, individuals may over-identify with their jobs, material achievement, and many other external sources interpreted incorrectly as empowerment, because they are not rooted in a sense of Self at their core. "The aim of individuation is nothing less than to divest the self of the false wrappings of the persona on the one hand, and of the suggestive power of primordial images on the other" (p. 174). Self-reflection is crucial. Deeply feeling and knowing oneself assists one in living in the truth of one's innate wholeness, the essence of one's whole identity. Once one has formulated an identity, defending one's personality is no longer necessary. One becomes self-assured and embraces one's true strengths. Everyone is in a constant state of regeneration, renewal, change, and improvement, journeying constantly towards healing their inner selves.

THE INTERVIEW

To conduct the interviews, we have asked each participant a series of questions concerning empowerment. Among these questions there are three areas of emphasis: Empowerment, Balance and Happiness. Please see Page 1 for the quiz.

CHAPTER 2
LITERATURE

HISTORICAL LITERATURE

In many cases, the written historical records reflect a mainly patriarchal perspective, due to women being primarily excluded from official history. With this said, we traced back various written works of literature that support the theories hypothesized by our research study. Demonstrating throughout history women have felt both empowered and suppressed. When suppressed, we see the need for women to regain the empowerment evident in earlier cultures.

Masculine and feminine. In the book *Have the Relationship You Want*, author Rori Raye describes feminine energy as encompassing being, feeling, expressing, experiencing, sensual, fun, and receiving; and masculine energy as doing, thinking, action-oriented, decision-making, logistics-handling, nurturing, and giving (Raye, 2006). At the onset of this book, a defining of masculine and feminine is integral to the underpinnings of this research.

According to Jung's ideas, we perceive how binarism between men and women moves according to pre-determined masculine and feminine energies. In China, the masculine and feminine are viewed as energy flowing between two poles. The Chinese symbol for the feminine is Yin, a receptive energy, and the masculine, expressed as Yang, is responsible for creative energy. The key between these polarities is the balanced "interaction and relationship" between the energies (Sanford, 1980, p. 8).

As philosopher Nicholas Berdyaev explains, "Man is not only a sexual but a bisexual being, combining the masculine and the feminine principle in himself (herself) in different proportions and often in fierce conflict. A man in whom the feminine principle was completely absent would be an abstract being, completely severed from the cosmic element. A woman in whom the masculine principle was completely absent would not be a personality.... It is only the union of these two principles that constitutes a complete human being. Their union is realized in every man and every woman within their bisexual, androgynous nature, and it also takes place through the intercommunion between the two natures, the masculine and the feminine." (1980, pp. 5–6)

Goddess traditions. Destiny is inviting women at this time in history to shake off old outworn personas and beliefs and step into the Sun, taking our rightful place again as Goddesses of the Earth. Women are constantly evolving, growing, throwing off perceived shackles and bindings, and coming into their own. The cyclical nature of time allows us to benefit from and recreate new storyboards from history. Thus, Goddess traditions provide a model and historical context of women's roles in society.

It is important to note that there is no unified academic conclusion concerning Goddess traditions. Rather, Downing (2004) said, theories span from being highly supportive to intensely dismissive of the various Goddess associations that Marija Gimbutas tied to archaeological findings. Of note, the questions involve the significance tied to female figurines whether they represent one actual Goddess, multiple Goddesses, or merely figures for sacred rituals. It is also important to understand whether dominant or equal roles were held by women.

The book *Goddesses in Art* (Graham, 1997) presents images depicting female strength and wisdom throughout history in Eastern and Western cultures. In the Old Stone Age, the Paleolithic, the Great Goddess was the image of fertility, giving and taking away life, represented in symbols of birth, death, and rebirth (pp. 9–10). In the New Stone Age, the Neolithic, the emphasis shifted to relationship, and the Goddess is usually depicted with a partner of equal or lesser stature, as in images of Mother Earth and Father Sky (p. 11). Graham states, "The Great Goddess was central to the minds and hearts of all Stone Age people, and she still is throughout the tribal world, from the Aborigines of Australia to the Kung of Africa" (p. 9). Moving into the Bronze Age, beginning about 5,000 years ago, the Goddess was conceived as part human and part animal and lived on a sacred mountain, the meeting place of heaven and earth (pp. 12-13). Western society and religion originated during the Iron Age that followed, from about 3,000 years ago, a time of primarily male-dominated societies, when male gods were favored over female goddesses. Specifically, the transition occurred as the Dorians in Greece and other Indo-Europeans elsewhere led invasions wielding iron weapons and replaced the goddess with their aggressive male divinities (Graham, 1997).

In Greek mythology, the Goddess Gaia, the divine earth mother, is the mother of all mothers. Chaotically birthed, a primal deity – she is associated with the cycles of life and fertility. She is regenerative, filled with psychic forces birthing mountains and unconscious dreams. "Her message is one of generous giving, of using the talents you've been blessed with to make the world a better place" (Riddle, 2013, p. 17). The divine powers of Gaia are both derived from earth and transcendent. "She is nature moving toward emergence in personal form.... She is shown as a human woman emerging breast high from the earth itself" (Downing, 1981/2007, p. 147). In an archetypal sense, Downing suggests, returning to the original Great Mother satisfies a deep inner longing for nurturing, reunites us with our oneness, and establishes a path for forgiveness of our paternal mother.

> Gaia really is mother; she mothers children; more importantly she mothers mothers. We are not called to be children in relation to her, but to be birth-givers – who make of every drop of semen or blood that falls on us something vital, though not necessarily something easily valued. (p. 155)

An ancient deity and creator, the Hindu goddess Tara, embodies two natures, encompassing White Tara's compassion and peace and Green Tara's boldness and fiercely protective spirit. In physical form, Tara is also a dichotomy gifted with the ability to appear as a human man, yet she chooses to remain as a woman. Tara's name means "star" or "she who brings forth life" in Sanskrit. In Buddhism, Tara is a female Buddha, "often called the Enlightened One" and "believed to be at one with every living thing, and like the Buddha, she is wise, spiritual, and loving" (Riddle, 2013, p. 40). "You can work with Tara to overcome problems and help you through stressful situations. You can call upon her benevolent nature, and ask her to soothe your soul. Her lesson is one of inner peace, and cleansing the spirit" (p. 41).

Another Mother Goddess is the Virgin Mary, a mother of Gods, the one who brought Christ to the world. "Beyond her is transcendence and consequently she represents that which is transcendent, as well as what is potential, what is in the future; she is the source and the end" (Campbell, 2013, p. 237). There are different times in history concerning the promotion of the Virgin Mary. *The Miracles of Our Lady,* Los Milagros de Nuestra Senora, by Gonzalo de Berceo, written around 1260, was a collection of miracles by the Blessed Virgin Mary written to promote Marian devotions. (Berceo, 2006) Although this is true for that period in history it is also relevant today. In the 21st century, there are Virgin Mary organizations with millions of members who pray to her for health and prosperity, such as the Legion of Mary and the Blue Army of Our Lady of Fatima.

Like the Virgin Mary, Kwan Yin, a Chinese Mother Goddess or mother of all Buddhas, is full of empathy, tenderness, and generosity; she assists the suffering, nurtures children, and assists women during childbirth. "Kwan Yin's message is one of unconditional love and compassion. She teaches us to treat others as we would wish to be treated, to show respect, and to offer a helping hand to those in need" (Riddle, 2013, p. 36).

Born of the Sky Goddess Nut and Earth God Geb, Isis is the Life Mother associated with nurturing love and rebirth. Egypt's most powerful goddess was a great sorceress of magic, holding infinite knowledge, relying fully on her intuition's guidance and ability to read individuals to successfully lead her people. Isis's strengths were her ability to communicate effectively and to connect with, care for, protect, and teach her people to "grow corn, weave, and use medicine." Isis demonstrates "the importance of knowledge, of learning and of broadening our horizons. Her power is in her ability to connect with people, and in having a keen sixth sense. She teaches us to trust our instincts" (Riddle, 2013, pp. 77-78).

Nonduality. During the time when the Goddess reigned as a deity, the feminine held great power and divinity and yet, the complementary social roles assigned women and men allowed for harmony.

Perhaps the most provocative discovery of recent archaeological research is that nowhere in Neolithic Goddess culture is there any sign of warfare. There is no evidence of fortifications, of violent death, invasion, or conquest. We can only conclude that there was some direct relation between Goddess religion and peaceful coexistence. Neolithic Goddess culture was women-centered, peaceful, prosperous, and nonhierarchical. (Gadon, 1989, p. 24)

Although his ideas may be refuted, we may acknowledge the primary peaceful role the Goddess had in society. In this sense, Riane Eisler, in *The Chalice and the Blade* (1987), identifies a theme of "power-with" in the Goddess culture, as opposed to the "power-over" of the God culture. Therefore, to embrace a "power-with" ideal enhances collaboration, community, earth-centeredness, and nonviolence. The worship of the Goddess as the primary deity will transition with the establishment of patriarchal societies.

The dominance of the masculine. The transition from the Goddess cultures to cultures where male gods predominate radically transformed society. The onset of iron-making and invasions was originally thought to create an evolutionary change. The transformation of culture occurred with the "emergence of agriculture," which introduced specifically the plow, which led to the transition from goddess civilizations to the "historical development" of established male-dominated societies (Lerner, 1986). Some feminists believe that excessive masculinity currently dominates our modern society due to the loss and repression of the Divine Feminine.

Archaic states are everywhere characterized by the emergence of property classes and hierarchies; commodity production with a high degree of specialization and organized trade over distance regions; urbanism; the emergency and consolidation of military elites; kinship; the institutionalization of slavery; a transition from kin dominance to patriarchal families as the chief mode of distributing goods and power. In Mesopotamia, there also occur important changes in the position of women: female subordination within the family becomes institutionalized and codified in law; prostitution becomes established and regulated; with increasing specialization of work, women are gradually excluded from certain occupations and professions. After the invention of writing and the establishment of formal learning, women are excluded from equal access to such education. The cosmogonies, which provide the religious underpinnings for the archaic state, subordinate female deities to chief male gods, and feature myths of origin which legitimate male ascendancy. (Lerner, 1986, p. 54)

The previous quote guides us to conclude that patriarchal supremacy lead to the rise of institutionalized violence. An idea shared by Shlain (2003), who believes that masculine energies are responsible for an overly aggressive culture and are simultaneously praised for technological advancements in society. The challenge that this poses to the collective is the increasing rate of aggression and violence. Thus it is determined that the patriarchal male-based society has imposed itself over several millenniums in the so-called Western society. The detachment from Goddess deities into male Gods not only lead to violence, but also a loss of humanity and meaning. In *Femininity Lost and Regained*, Johnson (1990, p. 90) notes that Western society's embrace of the masculine is reflected "in our linguistic poverty, in our lack of feeling for human relationships, and finally in our hunger for meaning, as meaning is the realm of the feminine" (p. 90). Similar beliefs are shared by Parrish-Harra, to whom,

The traits of excessive masculinity have moved into negative over-expression: competition without compassion, brute force, power without temperance, war without mercy or nobility and lack of respect and appreciation for emotion, nature and the life of the earth are all part of the absence of love for the Divine Feminine Principle. We must bring in the love that is needed in order to "thinketh in the heart." (Parrish-Harra, 1988, p. 20)

The current times have allowed us to re-embrace with our feminine self while simultaneously acknowledging the importance of balance.

We cannot let the pendulum of history to erase, but rather to reconcile the opposites.

Balance returns. As noted previously, Jung (1987) called the feminine inner personality in the unconscious of the male the anima, and the masculine personality in the unconscious of the female the animus. Shlain (2003) compares the Eastern philosophy of balanced yin and yang (masculine and feminine) with the primarily masculine, competitive nature of the West. Yin and yang, like animus and anima, are opposing yet complementary principles. An excess of either causes an unbalanced life, an aspect depicted as being a characteristic of our Western 21st century, for both men and women. In turn, the imbalance provokes the unhappiness of the individual in our society. Parrish-Harra (1988) affirms that moving back toward the feminine would reduce the negative impact of competition, power struggles, war, and lack of respect for emotion and nature. Integrating the masculine with the feminine, would strengthen, balance, and heal both men's and women's relationships with themselves and the collective.

> To relieve the isolation and confusion of modern man,
> to enable him to find his place in the great stream of life,
> to help him gain a wholeness which may knowingly and
> deliberately reunite his luminous conscious side with his
> dark unconscious side – this is the meaning and purpose of
> Jungian psychological guidance. (Jacobi, 1969/1973, p. 50)

Summary. Many of today's societal preoccupations deal with our internal conflicts, which in turn, affects our relationships, our communities, and even our planet. Thus, the lack of empathy and disarray has lead to the abuse of the earth and human resources. In order to heal us and to heal the world, it is time for a return to balance. With balance returning, the beneficial qualities emerging from integrating feminine and masculine traits will allow us to make whole all the dimensions of the Self. In the Cherokee sacred calendar, the number 2 represents the,

> Pulsation ray of Dual Polarity, the two opposites that
> also complement each other. The essence of the Universe
> is to balance these Sacred Twins: Good and Evil, Night
> and Day, Master and Slave, Black and White, Yin and Yang
> – Male and Female. Spirits maintain a perfect balance, and

are therefore neither male nor female. Cherokees dance to Balance the Earth; you have an invitation to The Dance. (Hail, 2000, p. 94)

The ability to cherish and respect each other's feminine and masculine inner side will create internal wholeness, reconnecting relationships with each other and the Mother Earth.

CHAPTER 3.
DISCOURSES AND WOMEN

THE BONES

Core concepts in analytical psychology as developed by Carl G. Jung provide a clinical foundation for this book. Jung, like all depth psychologists, worked on bringing the unconscious to consciousness by focusing on the symbolism presented in his clients' inner work. To his research and practice, Jung applied his background in Freudian theory and an interest in ancient literature, such as Sanskrit, mythology, religion, philosophy, Gnosticism, alchemy, mandala symbols, Kabala, Hinduism, and Buddhism. Jung viewed the human psyche as having three parts: *ego* or conscious mind, the personal unconscious, and the collective unconscious. In Jung's (1977) description of the human psyche, ego or conscious mind consists of the complexes, contents of archetypes, and is an envoy of the personality. The *shadow* is the area of the psyche that carries aspects of oneself one is ashamed of or afraid to claim. It is a part of the *personal unconscious*, which is organized by complexes, driving one toward individuation. The *collective unconscious*, characterized by archetypes traced in dreams and myths, consists of the continuum of experiences and knowledge shared by all human beings. Each of these parts of the human psyche contribute to the Self, defined as the whole archetypal organization of the individual, who, through symbolic thinking, is driven toward *individuation*. An *individuation* that culminates in wholeness, balance, and harmony.

Stages of individuation. Jung (1928/1972) categorizes individuation as self-realization; it "means precisely the better and more complete fulfillment of the collective qualities of the human being" (pp. 173-174). In Jungian theory, the path to individuation involves elucidating dreams, bringing the unconscious to consciousness, and journaling about the symbols and imagery and stories resonating in one's interior life. In other words, he proposes that in order to truly know oneself and achieve wholeness one must withdraw one's projections, do the inner work necessary to integrate all the parts of one's personality, and identify one's potential (Jung, 1953/1977).

By achieving equal expression of every aspect of the personality, the individual would be able to live harmoniously with others and with themselves in a nonselfish, true expression of a balanced psyche. This work requires engaging with the unconscious, which can pose particular difficulty for women in today's Western society.

> To recognize contents emerging from the unconscious is, therefore, of crucial importance to all people, particularly for women, who have been victimized for so many centuries by man's projections. Particularly today, when society is changing so rapidly, a woman may have a difficult time – knowing what and whom she is. Only by clarifying conditions and situations, and by distinguishing between subject and object, can a person begin to face and deal with reality. The greater the light shed on subliminal spheres within the psyche, the better equipped are the individuals to discriminate and understand the meaning and impact of those powers, which inundate and blind them, robbing them of their psychological independence. Clarification is difficult and frequently painful. It may lead to confrontation, but this may encourage people to come to grips with their projections – those troublesome powers they project unknowingly onto others because they either long to possess them or because they are plagued and hurt by them. (Knapp, 1987, p. 2)

Jung (1953/1977) believed that people naturally move through individuation as they mature, but may consciously intensify the process by actively shedding a light on the unconscious. This eases the tension inherent in this process by acknowledging its contents and accepting their true selves. He notes that this process begins by one's engagement with and unveiling of *shadow* material; the parts of one's self that one has split off, repressed, and does not acknowledge as one's own. The fear that lays under the surface, when one does not accept these traits as one's own, will be projected into one's environment or acted out in a symbolic manner. An individual who chooses to confront the *shadow* materials has the opportunity to consciously embrace it, rather than repressing it and acting out in damaging ways. The primary goal is to courageously shed light on the *shadow* material avoiding the suppression of unconscious elements and gaining access to a wellspring of valuable information. This process is extremely important for woman as Western society's projections penalize the authentic expression of Self.

In the second stage, a woman's individuation is achieved by embracing the animus, the unconscious masculine aspects of her psyche. On the contrary, men need to acknowledge their anima, or unconscious female aspects of their psyche. Unless one becomes aware and develops a relationship with the animus or anima, the shadow material will manifest as projections onto others, developing only half of one's potential (Jung, 1953/1977). Jung described the animus as the "soul-image" a functional complex requiring integration with the individual. An unconscious animus is likely to be aggressive and opinionated (Jung, 1928/1972). As a result, in many cases, the unconscious woman's animus often exaggerates male characteristics and the man's underlying anima may make him feel moody and feminine. Integrating the animus and anima in each other's respective sex has positive results. In women, as many articles have shown (Jung, 1957), the inner masculine becomes creative in woman. On the other hand, the inner feminine in men inspires their work.

Within this context, individuals often present a *persona*, an outwardly acceptable social mask, concealing their authentic selves. Jung believed individuals with a rigid mask or *persona* are disconnected from their natural state. Disassociation from the *persona*, ridding oneself of the social mask, is important to gain freedom and to move towards wholeness (Jung, 1972).

Another point in the process of individuation occurs when one discovers one's Self through an integration of outward and inner realities. This midpoint between the tension of the opposites brings the individual into wholeness. Truly knowing oneself is the call of women's self-realization leading to their empowerment. An idea shared by Jung (1928/1972) who states, "awareness of Self and full integration of all dimensions to encompass one's personality is the key to wholeness" (pp. 286-287).

The collective importance of women's empowerment. Studies demonstrate the overarching theme that empowered women benefit our society as a whole (Kristof & WuDunn, 2009). The role of empowered women promotes a healthy society. Foremost, maintaining a healthy relationship with the Self benefits not only the family's wellbeing, but also the community as a whole. Studies have proven an empowered woman will find ethical solutions to today's challenges, ranging from the environment, to engaging in conflict resolution, to mitigating social injustice (Kristof & WuDunn, 2009). Amartya Sen, the Indian Nobel laureate economist, claimed that a country's development depends primarily on women's involvement in all aspects of a country's culture, from economic to political (Myers, 2008).

Why is women's empowerment important and how does it contribute to the collective? Pulitzer Prize winners Nicolas Kristof and Sheryl WuDunn (2009) traveled the world giving a voice to gender inequality and the injustices done to women in their book Half the Sky, where they revealed that the key to transforming global poverty is women.

The World Bank's Chief Economist believes that in developing countries, the highest return on investment is a girl's education (Kristof & WuDunn, 2009). In the past, Indian Nobel laureate economist Amartya Sen (Myers, 2008) focused primarily on basic needs for women's empowerment, nevertheless, they comprehended that to create a long-term impact they needed to focus also on education, finance, and property.

Research completed by the United Nations Development Programme states that women's empowerment assists a country in economic productivity, reduces infant mortality rates, improves overall health and nutrition, and increases access to education for the family (Kristof & WuDunn, 2009). For instance, the founder of Doctors Without Borders, French Foreign Minister Bernard Kouchner, agreed that empowering women will benefit the future (Kristof & WuDunn, 2009).

Around the world, many countries that previously treated their women as burdens and as commodities to be sold and bartered are beginning to tap into women as valuable natural resources to support the economic stability of their countries. Kristof and WuDunn (2009) noted that China is an example of a country that benefitted financially from women entering the workforce and making different life choices regarding family planning.

United Nations former secretary general Kofi Annan (Myers, 2008) stated women have always played the role of peacemakers in their homes and continue to be excellent mediators in their communities. They are "instrumental in building bridges rather than walls" (p. 110). Politically, women tend to support bills benefitting families, our environment, and social reform (Myers, 2008). Rwanda's president, Paul Kagame (Kristof & WuDunn, 2009), instituted policies to maintain a 30% female parliament, thus empowering and promoting women because of their demonstration of responsibility and nonviolence during the genocides. As a result, studies say that Rwanda overcame unethical government practices for the first time in decades. UN Women states, "More women in politics does not necessarily correlate with lower levels of corruption, as is often assumed. Rather, democratic and transparent politics is correlated with low levels of corruption, and the two create an enabling environment for more women to participate." (UN Women, 2015)

In 2008, Norway was the leader in countries' national legislatures with large percentages of women, followed by Rwanda's 55% female legislators, Sweden, Finland, and Costa Rica. The United States was ranked 68th with 17% female legislators, and the countries with the least women were Saudi Arabia, Qatar, Kyrgyzstan, Yemen, and Egypt (Kristof & WuDunn, 2009; Myers, 2008). Almost a decade later, Rwanda leads the pack with the highest number of women parliamentarians, the Nordic countries following in second, Americas and Europe in close proximity, sub-Saharan Africa, then Asia, Middle and North Africa, and the Pacific, based on data from the Inter-Parliamentary Union. (UN Women, 2015)

Fortune 500 companies benefit financially from having women on their boards. Catalyst performed a study across all industries resulting in statistics demonstrating companies with the highest percentage of women have a 53% higher return on equity, 42% higher return on sales, and 66% higher return on investment capital (Myers, 2008).

Nevertheless, along with the economic growth that women represent to society, we have to care for the inner soul and disregard the negative aspects that Western society has imposed on women. Finding inner balance plus opportunities for women will transform and help our planet.

A double-edged sword: Women's internal experience. From a psychological, societal, and economic standpoint, we have seen how beneficial it is to empower the world's women. Yet, as the dedication to women's empowerment grows, also women must overcome negative internal and external messages in order to increase self-esteem. One of the aspects that holds women back in today's society, is that women believe they have no value (Hay, 1997). Due to childhood experiences and societal conditioning, many women have low self-esteem based on the belief that their role is to take care of others and that their feelings and interests are secondary (Hay, 1997).

Playing a role in creating positive change in the world depends on women coming to accept whom they are and the great value they hold (Hay, 1997). Women need to overcome their self-doubts and appreciate the unique gifts they each have to bestow on the world. What each woman will find as she courageously steps out to pursue her interests, to speak her mind, is that she has been good enough and even better than she expected all along (Myers, 2008).

Research has confirmed that our belief system does affect our self-esteem. Numerous studies have shown that our beliefs, thoughts, and words directly influence the outcome of our lives. Adopting a positive belief system increases good experiences reinforcing positive beliefs. Vice versa, an individual's negative belief system promotes the possibility of increasingly bad experiences (Hay, 1997).

In a study, cited by Myers, researchers attempted to understand the factors influencing gender stereotypes. The research addressed the following question: Can you override stereotypes by getting people to think about their strengths? The answer was a resounding "yes." In this study, the psychologists chose the Vanderberg Mental Rotation spatial test, where men typically perform better then women. The researchers divided 90 college students split evenly between men and women into three groups. Each group received a different research question and then took the test. Group 1's question was generic and men scored on average better than women did. Group 2's question reminded the participants of their specific gender and women performed substantially worse than men. Group 3's questions to the participants were to think of their strengths and surprisingly men and women's scores were on par with each other (Myers, 2008). Then we can see based on this study, women are affected by the perception of gender roles. The projections of society to gender roles and the resistance to them have failed to take into account the inner wellbeing of women. In some cases, the lack of fulfillment of women's inner selves impedes women from expressing themselves in a true manner, therefore failing to achieve womanhood. The internal factor that impedes women's progress, in response to women's changing roles in society, is an animus-possession. We conclude that women's outward success has left them in power, yet confused, resentful, and unhappy.

Upon entering the male-dominated workforce, women typically chose two different paths: Either, mirroring and exaggerating the characteristics of their successful male counterparts or exaggerating the traditionally feminine mannerisms. At both poles, neither of the roles feels authentic and women are left feeling at odds with themselves. One of the reasons, why women may try to overcompensate their animus is the feeling that the feminine role is not taken seriously (Myers, 2008). On the contrary, in some cases women may be overtly sexualized as an object as a means of gaining trust eluding the threat of visibility.

However, women are beginning to see that an entirely masculine or feminine approach is neither beneficial to themselves or to those with whom they interact. The CEO of BET, Deborah Lee, decided to stop managing like a man "in order to be true to herself and benefit the company" (Myers, 2008, p. 92). Lee transitioned from imitating a male CEO to realizing that her true authenticity would provide increased gains for both herself and the organization.

Similarly, Hillary Clinton has shared her struggles with attempting to find a balance that allows her to convey strength and not aggression (Myers, 2008). Through this journey to find the right balance, Clinton endeavored to convey confidence and compassion as a political figure. In Diane Sawyer's Public and Private interview, Hillary Clinton reflected on being in the spotlight as a woman:

Because when you're in the spotlight as a woman, you know you're being judged constantly. I mean, it is just never-ending. You get a little worried about, 'Okay, you know, people over on this side are loving what I'm wearing, looking like, saying. And people over on this side aren't.' Your natural tendency is how do you bring people together so you can better communicate. I'm done with that. I mean, I'm just done. I am over it. I think I have changed. To not worry so much about what other people are thinking. My view is I have lived an incredibly blessed life. I have had so many wonderful experiences. And I am going to say what I know, what I believe, and let the chips fall. (Clinton, 2014)

Former Press Secretary Dee Dee Myers, in *Why Women Should Rule the World*, pondered today's women's roles in society, "Too male. Not male enough. Too female. Not female enough" (2008, p. 47). Myers felt a great deal of pressure as the first woman White House Press Secretary. Finding a middle ground between being likable and authoritative was often difficult for her (Myers, 2008). During Hillary Clinton's 2008 campaign concerning gender and sexism, she said:

I was not as effective calling it out during that campaign either because there is a double standard, we live with a double standard.... And I think part of what I did not do was to be more clear in saying, "Look, this is a problem in our country. And people oughtta think about their own daughters, their own sisters, their own mothers when they make comments about women in public life, whether they're in politics or the media or anywhere else." (Clinton, 2014)

Ideally, Hillary Clinton speaks of working to find "just the right balance," and Dee Dee Myers says her success depended on discovering "a more effective middle ground." Hillary and Dee Dee are both sharing their struggle with attempting to discover a balance that is more personal. The aim is adaptability. Adaptability is required in order to behave appropriately based on the specific situation. Therefore, for women and men, integrating the animus or anima may be positive based on the situation. Professionally, the animus assists a woman with focusing on goals and achievements, and, personally, the anima helps a man with caring for family, friends and the individuals around him. Female and male psychological traits are a large measure interchangeable in both men and women.

A double-edged sword: Women's external experience. Women's potency in the world is affected by internal messages whose origins are both externally and internally based. Whereby, the external messages influence her development of worth, which in turn reinforces her self-doubt. One of the aspects that affect internal thoughts are externally imposed factors, ranging from the lack of opportunities to inequality in pay. Women need more opportunities to advance onward to senior positions within organizations, and yet they receive less compensation for their equal contributions to men. Prior to negotiating pay and position, Pew Research Center said women graduating from college make 93 cents to their male counterparts' dollar. Over time the gap increases, averaging only an 84% of the male earnings (Adamczyk, 2014).

As women overcome their negative internal messages, external obstacles continue to obstruct their path. Organizations typically believe family responsibilities account for fewer women in the higher ranks of organizations. Based on corporate research, lack of opportunity and dissatisfaction are a bigger factor in women leaving corporate jobs (Myers, 2008). Mike Cook, past president of Deloitte & Touché, noticed that although they were hiring equal numbers of men and women within the organization, there were few women in executive roles. He initiated an internal study to interview women who had left the company during the past 10 years to discover the missing link. The results of the research were that women were left out of career planning discussions and that the decisions were made for them based on gender selection for roles. If a position involved extensive travel or was in a male-dominated field, the organization excluded the women, who in turn felt opportunities were limited (Myers, 2008).

Professionally, women's success depends on opportunities for advancement, the appropriate resources to fulfill her obligations, and the equal authority to her responsibility. Victoria Medvec of the Center for Executive Women at Northwestern University's Kellogg School of Management concluded that women undermine themselves by their inability to negotiate for the resources and tools they need for success (Myers, 2008).

Another key external challenge for women is equal acknowledgment for their contributions. Studies continue to demonstrate inequality in pay scales between men and women and "data showed that women earned 44 percent less than men" in research conducted by the U.S. General Accountability Office (Myers, 2008, p. 27). In November 2010, the Senate voted "no" on the Paycheck Fairness Act designed to bridge the pay scale gap between women and men. The bill would have provided enhancements to the Equal Pay Act of 1963, whose intention was to create equal pay for men and woman and more legal rights. The Paycheck Fairness Act was reintroduced in 2011, 2012, 2014, and 2015 and blocked each time by the Senate.

Radford University psychology professor Hilary Lips conducted research by career type. Her study further demonstrated the inequality between men's and women's pay scales. The results of her study were that men received significantly more compensation in every job category, including in typically women's fields such as secretarial and nursing. Lips concluded that the research results lead one to think that any job position is less valuable with a woman in the role (Myers, 2008).

Women's empowerment is on the rise, yet, to truly flourish, women need to have access to information, critical resources and equal value given to their work. Therefore, society needs to provide women more options for advancement, to extend the necessary resources available to them, and provide the proper authority that enables them to be successful in their chosen roles. Nevertheless, women are responsible for their progress and need to hold themselves accountable by asking for financial support, opportunities, and graciously promoting their successes (Myers, 2008). Women need to know their worth, select roles matching their values, and ask for the support they require.

Superwoman complex.

No book has yet been written in praise of a woman who let her husband and children starve or suffer while she invented even the most useful things, or wrote books, or expressed herself in art, or evolved philosophic systems. (Spencer, 1908, p. 82)

Women need to create a balance between their personal and professional roles that fits their time requirements, financial goals, and emotional needs. When balance suffers, women suffer, and then everyone suffers. "In a huge effort to keep everything in the household, the relationship, and our daily lives running along smoothly, and in an even bigger effort to keep our resentment and anger quiet and hidden we overfunction" (Raye, 2006, p. 118).

Many women today are the caretakers of everyone within their sphere of influence. The general view seems to be that the ability to self-reflect and convey their needs is less important. Superwoman attempts to save everyone except herself. The Superwoman limits herself through her fear, believing she will not meet others' expectations nor her own, followed by the inevitable guilt when she does not succeed. She continuously adds more responsibility, heavily holding her close to the ground impeding the ability to fly (Thoele, 1988/1991).

How does a Superwoman overfunction and how can she embrace her humanness? "Overfunctioning is doing too much. It's doing more than your fair share, doing other [people's] work, and helping where no help is needed. It's stepping in when you know you could do a better job, stepping up to rescue someone, jumping in to save the situation" (Raye, 2006, p. 117). In this sense, the masculine attributes of setting boundaries and limits avoids overfunctioning, therefore creating a healthy balance in one's life.

Overfunctioning is rooted in a lack of self-esteem. A sentiment that underlies the thought that she is not "good enough." She attempts to compensate through being excessively "nice" while doing more than her share to prove she is loveable. However, in truth, a woman with reasonable boundaries, who appreciates her self-worth, and does not accept inferior or poor treatment, is a better role model than Superwoman (Raye, 2006).

The current push for women's empowerment is as much a blessing as it is a curse. We can compare women's current challenges using an airline analogy, where you have to secure your own oxygen mask before assisting others with theirs. As we have seen, women tend to overfunction, failing to help themselves first therefore ultimately failing to assist others. The mental and physical health of women should be the primary goal. A healthy woman who values her health is the new role model.

A goal for women would be to move away from the overfunctioning of a Superwoman. We have to shout "Superwoman Doesn't Live Here Anymore!" As women allow themselves to be human *be-ings* "committed to improvement we [can] begin to untie the ropes that bind us" (Thoele, 1988/1991, p. 26).

Personal/professional balance. Moving away from feeling the obligation to overfunction, women begin to accept their humanness and their ability to just BE. With this movement toward health, they can say no to overfunctioning, enabling them, through self-respect, to choose the right opportunities.

Former White House Press Secretary Dee Dee Myers is an example of a woman who transitioned from overfunctioning towards honoring her authentic self. As the White House Press Secretary Myers felt burned out, she had been working 80 hours a week, she knew it was imperative for her personal sanity to reduce her hours by moving into a position with more flexibility. With this knowledge, she was able to create her dream job, which combines time on a political show, writing, and as a public speaker. According to Myers (2008), she fulfilled her dreams.

The life/work balance approach is a factor developing in today's society. Numerous organizations are offering flexibility and more options. "A recent study of seventy-two large U.S. firms showed that family-friendly policies increased the number of women in senior management positions in subsequent years" (Myers, 2008, p. 167).

Moreover, balancing personal and professional aims crosses gender lines. "In a recent Fortune magazine survey, 84 percent of men said they'd like more time outside of work, and more than half said they'd be willing to sacrifice income to get it" (Myers, 2008, p. 160). Organizations are responding to this cultural change. Organizations such as Discovery Communications offer telecommuting, flexible hours, and on-site health care (Myers, 2008). Life/work balance is continuing to grow as organizations offer flexible schedules and extend their paid parental leave benefits in an effort to attract and retain top talent. Organizations such as Netflix, Amazon, Google and Facebook are changing with the times to accommodate the employee's preferences. (Adamczk, 2015) "The U.S. still lags behind other countries when it comes to paid parental leave. In 2014, the International Labour Organization revealed that among the 185 countries reviewed, only the United States and Papua New Guinea did not have public policies for paid maternity leave. The report also found that 78 of those countries also mandated paternity leave, with 70 of those providing paid leave to new fathers." (Dishman, 2015)

In the 21st century, when much of the economy is in a downturn, women-owned businesses continue to be a growth segment. Many women have stepped away from large corporations and out of positions that no longer hold meaning for them. Women are beginning to build something more intimate and personal for themselves. This is partially achieved through the application of new technology and the cultural acceptance of it. Women and men have the flexibility to create their own career paths in alignment with their values and interests. We will continue to see improvements in this area, as inner values become part of a new currency.

As women eliminate the need to overfunction, identify their priorities, and create situations that align with their highest values, the impact will benefit themselves, their families, and their respective communities. Meredith Yieira, former co-host of the Today show, is an example of a woman who re-evaluated her priorities in order to empower herself. When she left the position, other women questioned her economic ethics, based on the assumption that money and power in a patriarchal society equals happiness. Yieira conveyed being true to herself by acknowledging the importance of quality time with her family. According to Myers (2008), she never regretted the decision.

Extremes of the masculine and feminine.

When we observe the way in which women, since the second half of the nineteenth century, have begun to take up masculine professions, to become active in politics, to sit on committees, etc., we can see that woman is in the process of breaking with the purely feminine sexual pattern of unconsciousness and passivity, and has made a concession to masculine psychology establishing herself as a visible member of society. (Jung, 1982, p. 59)

Although, some of Jung's approaches toward gender roles have aged, we can still utilize the portions of his theories that are still relevant. In the 1930s, Jung saw the difficulties that women taking part in traditionally male professional roles could face. In this context, Jung foresaw that by moving into a male-dominated world, women emulate some of the male projected behaviors, therefore losing a part of their own feminine identity. Jung's animus and anima concepts may help us understand men's and women's evolution beyond traditionally patriarchal defined gender roles.

Patriarchally and conventionally biased, Jung discourages the women's movement and expounds a woman's expression as neurotic. Yet, by appropriating and modifying his thoughts, we can apply certain of his theories in a different manner. In this sense, we agree that women and men should consciously develop their *animus* and *anima* in varying degrees to achieve balance.

> We all are a mix of Masculine and Feminine energies, the Feeling and the Thinking, the Being and the Doing.... At our best, we move back and forth fluidly between Masculine Doing energy and Feminine Being energy. Most of us experience ourselves stuck in Masculine energy. We've taken on the Doing of the world – in fact many of us feel as though we are actually *holding up* our world. (Raye, 2006, pp. 119-120)

When in typically male professional roles, women try to overcompensate by bringing forward their *animus*. This is "how it happens that a professional woman lives her animus. The professional situation is new for woman and needs a new adaptation, and this, as always, is readily supplied by the animus" (Jung, 1982, p. 111). Extremes of the masculine creates internal disharmony disrupting a women's relationship with Self. Women overcompensate in their attempts to reproduce male role models and achievement values, and forget that their true value is in being, and thus they lose their sense of themselves (Campbell, 1990). The true essence of feminine energy is to "be," whereas masculine energy is about "doing." Joseph Campbell goes on to say a woman's "power is in their body and in their being and in their presence" (p. 101). When a woman loses touch with her true sense of power and instead imitates her interpretation of male energy, then the,

> Mental masculinization of the woman has unwelcome results. She may perhaps be a good comrade to a man without having any access to his feelings. The reason is

that her animus has stopped up the approaches to her own feeling. (Jung, 1982, p. 61)

A woman who is out of balance and overcompensates with her achievement-driven *animus* loses her femininity and destroys her relationships (Campbell, 1990). As described earlier, the consequence of a woman living exclusively from her *animus* is blockage from her feelings. The animus, also defined as the paternal Logos, resides in the background, whereby a woman unconsciously living her inferior animus in the foreground is the impetus for the masculinization of women. On the other hand, women can benefit from consciously developing the inner masculine of her feminine personality, therefore balancing her inner forces (Jung, 1982). Rather than a woman unconsciously reacting from the animus, consciously integrating her animus develops a healthy internal relationship with the Self.

The source of the adverse effects to men and women is the imbalance of both genders, resulting alchemically in a new combustible substance that creates a tension within the Self and towards others. Living unconsciously through the anima and animus causes imbalance, disharmony, and animosity between the genders and culminates in community tension and lack of agreement.

In order to benefit humanity, each individual needs to engage in self-reflection and compassion. For instance, Jung offers the process of making the unconscious conscious to reduce the adverse effects of the animosity between the *anima* and *animus*.

A woman possessed by the animus is always in danger of losing her femininity, her adapted feminine *persona*, just as a man in like circumstances runs the risk of effeminacy. These psychic changes of sex are due entirely to the fact that a function which belongs on the inside has been turned outside. (1982, p. 98)

In the 21st century, women and men are often unconsciously living out an unconscious contrasexual archetype. Thanks to the feminist movements, women have been able to gain many of the needed liberties they were lacking. Yet, one of the trends that explore these new liberties has placed the *animus* in the foreground as a cultural current, therefore creating a unisexual culture. This is shown in the ambiguity in the depiction of sex identity to clothing. Having the *animus* and *anima* in mind, we will have to wait to see the possible cultural outcomes of this trend.

To expand further, humans must learn to encompass the full spectrum of masculine and feminine traits. A conscious relation to a woman's inner masculine and a man's inner feminine is healthy. Otherwise, unconsciously being ruled by an unconscious archetype places the individual in crisis, because the unconsciously driven primitive self is unnatural for the personality (Jung, 1982). When an individual lives unconsciously, psychic demands cloud and disturb the consciousness. That is, the *primitive* self comes to the foreground when the inner world remains unconscious.

Therefore, the initial step to healing society is moving with intention and making the unconscious conscious, within each individual. Jung justifies "deliberate attention should then be given to the unconscious so that the compensation can set to work…. For their power grows in proportion to the degree that they remain unconscious. Those who do not see them are in their hands" (Jung, 1982, p. 178).

It is by intentionally bringing forward the contents of the unconscious to the surface that an individual has the capacity to identify helpful from disruptive attributes. This process assists the individual in selecting and melding together advantageous traits to create a balanced personality.

Because the things of the inner world influence us all the more powerfully for being unconscious, it is essential for anyone who intends to make progress in self-culture (and does not all culture begin with the individual?) to objectivate the effects of the anima and then try to understand what contents underlie those effects. In this way he adapts to, and is protected against, the invisible. No adaptation can result without concessions to both worlds. From a consideration of the claims of the inner and outer worlds, or rather, from the conflict between them, the possible and the necessary follows. Unfortunately our Western mind, lacking all culture in this respect, has never yet devised a concept, nor even a name, for the *union of opposites through the middle path*, that most fundamental item of inward experience, which could respectably be set against the Chinese concept of Tao. Is it at once the most individual fact and the most universal, the most legitimate fulfillment of the meaning of the individual's life. (Jung, 1982, p. 94)

To achieve Tao or optimal balance, women being uniquely individual, some women require the discipline to consciously integrate their latent masculine attributes and other women, who have unconsciously repressed their feminine values, will need to reclaim a relationship with their femininity.

Only with great difficulty have women extricated themselves from the feminine role which history prescribed for them and learned a new self-respect and independence. But this lesson could only be acquired by keeping their feelings strictly under control. All their energies have been engaged in developing the masculine side of their natures, and nothing meantime has been done toward disciplining and developing the feminine instinct which yet remains a most powerful force within them. (Harding, 1970, p. 77)

Rather than restraining and repressing her authentic feelings leading to urgent and dogmatic passions, a woman who gradually develops the ability to consciously and spontaneously express her instinctual feminine innermost feeling nature is a joy to behold. A woman who elicits the attitude of being in the world, but not of it, engages life purposefully from the masculine, and yet remaining deeply connected to her feminine feeling space. She moves through the world feeling empowered and happy, honoring her deepest needs.

A woman's creation is not an abstraction; it is a very personal thing, based primarily on her own subjective experience and not on objective experiences of the external world. If a woman is to create in a man's world, she needs not only to bring up into consciousness her masculine qualities, but also to experience deeply her feminine nature. (Harding, 1970, p. 81)

We conclude that an individual with increased consciousness and who observes their own behaviors and moods integrates the knowledge they have gained, benefiting from the new insights that were previously unavailable and leading, therefore, a more conscious life.

Symbols of the center: Mandalas and circles.

An Indian Chief said, "When we pitch camp, we pitch a camp in a circle. When the eagle builds a nest, the nest is a circle. When we look at the horizon, the horizon is in a circle." (Campbell, 1988, p. 214)

Symbols of the center represent how numerous traditions and cultures use symbols of oneness and nonduality interchangeably to represent the highest states of psychological achievement. The correlation between symbols of oneness and "subjective well-being" is relevant as each participant in the next chapter had an opportunity to express how their images of balance and wholeness related to their feelings of empowerment and happiness.

In Taoism, Hinduism, and Buddhism, the Goddess remains sacred, and these three ancient religions share a similar integral philosophy. In each respective religion, the masculine penetration of the feminine activates a genesis, from which everything is derived. Many of these depictions of the genesis use similar patterns of symbols, where men are circles (the infinite that activates) and women are squares (the material world that is activated by the penetration of the eternal). The description of the two shows a circle within a square, representing "the nonduality of god and goddess, heaven and earth, spirit and matter" (Graham, 1997, p. 21).

The Jungian scholar, Jolande Jacobi, also discusses the symbolic significance of the circle and square:

Their basic design is a circle or square symbolizing "wholeness", and in all of them the relation to a centre is accentuated......'pictures' of completed individuation i.e., the successful union of all the pairs of psychic opposites...... more or less successful steps toward ultimate perfection and wholeness. To strive for this goal is our destiny and highest calling....The mandalas with their mathematical structure are pictures, as it were, of the 'primal order of the total psyche', and their purpose is to transform chaos into cosmos. For these figures not only express order, they also bring it about. (Jacobi, 1969/ 1973, pp. 136-139)

Historically, the circle or square mandala is an ancient religious symbol, used as early as the Paleolithic age. Distinctly, Pueblo Indians, Tibetan Buddhists, and many cultures used mandalas for various practices such as ceremonial, meditation, and rites of passage. The Sanskrit word for circle is mandala, which means cosmic order. The intention of a Buddhist mandala is to coordinate your personal world within the cosmos, rearranging your circle within a larger circle. You may place a deity in the center, a deity that corresponds with the Self. The center is surrounded by peripheral images representing the deity's radiance (Campbell, 1988). Within the bigger circle, that represents the Cosmos, usually some peripheral images or objects of the individual's life are placed. In this context, Campbell explains that you draw the various value systems within your life in the circle to discover your center. "Making a mandala is a discipline for pulling all those scattered aspects of your life together, for finding a center and ordering yourself to it. You try to coordinate your circle with the universal circle...to be at the center" (p. 217).

Navajo Indians use mandala sand paintings for healing ceremonies, where the patient moves into the center to identify himself with universal symbolized power. In meditation, Tibetan monks use sand paintings "drawing cosmic images to represent the force of the spiritual powers that operate in our lives... to try to center one's life with the center of the universe... by way of mythological imagery" (Campbell, 1988, p. 217). Symbols of the circle are evident across the world, such as the masks of the Northwest Coast Indians, mandalas in Nepal, dance rituals of Krishna, sun disks in New Guinea, the rose window of the Chartres Cathedral, or the circular art created on buffalo skin by the Plains Indians. Campbell said, "The whole world is a circle. All of these circular images reflect the psyche, so there may be some relationship between these architectural designs and the actual structuring of our spiritual functions" (1988, p. 214). In this sense, the significance of symbols worldwide shows there is a correlation between the center and healing properties. We concur with these traditional cultures and their symbolic values of "the center." By overcoming polarization of the extremes we can unify the Self.

HAPPINESS.

Attaining wholeness, as described through traditional cultural rituals, involves harmonizing with the center. The goal of attaining wholeness mirrors the psychological, philosophical, religious, traditional, symbolic, and aesthetic ideologies afore mentioned, emphasizing transcending opposites.

The beneficial effects of balancing feminine and masculine attributes are confirmed in Ariel's *Bluebird Women and the New Psychology of Happiness* (Gore, 2010). She explores the question of whether a woman can be smart, empowered, and happy. Within the framework of her research, she found that the happiest women were those who demonstrated an openness to receive (feminine) and an ability to set boundaries (masculine). In addition, out of all the women interviewed, Ariel claims that the ones with a spiritual practice reported a higher degree of happiness than women who were agnostic or atheist. Factors such as having children or the lack thereof and marital status did not determine whether a woman was more or less happy.

Markedly, the happiest women share in common the themes of self-esteem, basic resources, making decisions based on their values, having reasonable boundaries, and saying no to expectations. They were optimists, open to new paths, and willing to grow and evolve as human *be-ings*, regardless of demographics (Gore, 2010). Specifically, Gore's research "predicted [that] happiness, then, was a kind of openness – a childlike curiosity coupled with a very grown-up understanding of self-respect and self-protection" (pp. 173-174). In addition, the research discredits the misconception that external factors lead to happiness. Instead, she affirms that individuals can positively influence their well-being through honing certain typically female (openness) and male (boundary setting) characteristics. The qualities of openness, self-respect, and self-protection are key predictors in the search for happiness.

Transitioning from the purely theoretical to the practical, how does a woman integrate the feminine and masculine in her daily life in order to invest in her personal satisfaction and happiness? Hypothetically, a woman balances "Feminine Energy: Being, Feeling, Expressing, Experiencing, Sensual, Fun, Receiving" with "Masculine Energy: Doing, Thinking, Action-Oriented, Decision-Making, Logistics-Handling, Nurturing, Giving" (Raye, 2006, p. 92).

Rather than an individual rigidly identifying with his or her biological sex or living out an inferior function, the intention is to merge, in the adequate amount, parts of the feminine and masculine characteristics within an individual. Moreover, individuals are psychologically and spiritually androgynous, reflecting their ability to express any number of qualities ranging in the sphere from masculine to feminine. Specifically, the individuals who adapt to the demands of any situation by modifying their behaviors, regardless of predetermined roles, are more emotionally healthy.

In order to clarify, we need to make a differentiation between the feminine and the masculine. To define "feminine energy is the exact opposite of the high octane, going and doing, stress-led life. It's about intuition, sensuality, fun, feeling, expressing. If Masculine energy is about doing, Feminine energy is about being. So what would it be like to just be?" (Raye, 2006, p. 92).

Once we have differentiated between feminine and masculine, we also have to concentrate on what women need in terms of their feminine and masculine, in varying degrees.

Women who are living out of their inferior function with an excess of animus need to connect with their femininity. A woman's authenticity is rooted in her ability to relax, be vulnerable, and trust in herself. The practice of self-trust enables women to relax and accept moment-by-moment that all is well within her world. Essentially, embracing the feminine involves trusting your intuition, being receptive to life, and expressing a compassionate nature towards yourself and your environment.

One of the tools available to women that aims to approach a relationship with her *animus*, is Raye's practical method of integrating the attributes of the masculine:

> Having boundaries means standing up for yourself in a simple, straightforward, and respectful way.... Saying No to what you don't want in order to be able to say Yes to what you do want will make an amazing difference – not only in the relationship (to others), but in the way you feel about yourself....You'll begin to see that some of your resentment and anger isn't about (others). You may be jealous of some freedom or flexibility (others have). As soon as you get that your feelings are about you not taking

care of yourself, your resentment will fade and you'll get determined to find those Nos and Yeses and follow through. (Raye, 2006, pp. 127–129)

The ultimate goal to empower women and to promote their happiness is Jung's process of making the unconscious conscious. It may be achieved by identifying the elements working under the surface, distinguishing helpful from disruptive attributes, and embracing advantageous traits, all culminating in a cosmic union of feminine and masculine elements. Thus, specific beneficial qualities emerge from the balancing of feminine and masculine traits, which predicates on the individual's personality, situations, and the degree of integration required.

CHAPTER 4
PSY 301: EMPOWERMENT & HAPPINESS

PSY 301: EMPOWERMENT & HAPPINESS

The phenomenological hermeneutic perspective, utilizing the method of narrative analysis from one-on-one interviews, has proved to be an effective process allowing for description, narrative analysis, and hermeneutic interpretation. Hence, the concluding phenomenological description of the themes and patterns found in the following interviews continues a logical sequence, while receptive to unexpected remarkable discoveries and findings.

In the interviews, the meaning of empowerment was clearly different for each individual. Yet, these empowered women shared common descriptions of what empowerment and happiness meant for them personally. These common distinct themes may be identified as the following: (a) survival mode versus (b) unconditional love, and the (c) integration of feminine and masculine energies.

As an illustration of survival mode, all participants reported that the Western definition of achievement and success leads to fear, survival, and regret for women. Based on the interviews, the participants believe women are doing what they have to do in order to survive and to provide a better life to their children. This progression culminates in women wanting the best for their daughters and a better life for their children; a life better than the one they experienced. The interviews show that the women believed they had focused incorrectly on success, and had paid a hard price for an interesting career and financial reward. These choices came at the expense of their and their children's happiness, realizing that choosing happiness is more important. Additionally, the participants' age also played a significant role in the self-assessment responses to the research questions. Specifically, the younger participants feared they would not have happy marriages and children, choosing to focus on their careers and financial stability. In retrospect, the eldest of the participants expressed regret that they had focused on success and career and stated they would do things differently if had the opportunity. Yet, they now felt too limited by age, money, and proximity to retirement to pursue a different dream.

Moreover, the theme of survival mode included the dominate subthemes detailed as (a) stress, (b) control, (c) "Superwoman Complex," and (d) financial obligations. For example, all participants reported stress from attempting to balance working a full-time job and management of the household. Those issues range from control, to the "Superwoman Complex," and to financial obligations restricting desires. All further adversely affecting the participants' well-being.

All participants felt stress from working two full-time roles: their professional work and the management of the household. Daily responsibilities demand their full attention, which triggered stress in all of the participants. Notably, the majority of participants felt frequent stress and expressed throughout the interviews control issues. These were mentioned multiple times by the participants as the necessity to maintain control over their environment. Their need to control their surroundings, in order to feel secure, affected negatively the participants since life is in a constant state of flux and unpredictability. The control issues caused by insecurity lead these women into a survival mode that is specific to the 21st century.

Similarly, pervading the psychology of modern women, the "Superwoman Complex" is a recurring theme among the majority of participants. The participants seemed to hold themselves to unreasonable expectations and levels of perfection that are unachievable on a daily basis by a human being. Finally, survival mode further influenced the majority of the participants as financial obligations restricted them from pursuing their ideal careers and interests. Even, a minority of the participants reported that "their life did not support them," meaning that the activities making up their daily life did not align with what they needed or wanted. Yet, let us clarify that these expectations are interpersonal, not financial.

Alternatively, participants reported that empowerment and happiness resulted from transitioning out of survival mode to an emphasis on unconditional love while integrating their feminine and masculine energies. All participants identified the necessity to focus on the love of self, family, friends, community, and the world as their key to a healthy balanced life. By way of example, the initial intention of love is to consciously direct one's "superconscious" toward love of self (self-love), then love of others, and love of the world. In particular, all participants expressed their belief that women are responsible for their own happiness and have the ability to make their own destiny.

The majority of participants stated that since early childhood, the practice of self-love begins with self-confidence, demonstrating self-sufficiency, and surrounding oneself with positive mentors. These character traits lead to mastery as an empowered woman. Moreover, early confidence building contributes to healthy self-esteem, enabling one to find the courage to demonstrate self-mastery. Parents, grandparents, friends, and mentors act as role models, providing the support to the participants to achieve a feeling of empowerment.

Continuing through life, an individual's daily practice of self-love is expressed in the ability to feed, nurture, and take care of oneself. In this sense, a key component of self-love is an individual feeling deserving and worthy of such pristine attention without self-criticism, judgment, expectations, and requirements of perfection. A few participants, in response to one interview question, articulated that women should place themselves first, give themselves the best, and not withhold from themselves what they are trying to provide for their children.

All participants agreed that setting healthy boundaries is appropriate, and the majority of participants stated that they required more time for self to just "be," in order to feel more happy and empowered. Additionally, half the participants stated that it is important to feel worthy of taking the time for the self, including vacations to increase happiness. Each of these items speaks to the critical nature of leading a balanced life in order to feel a higher overall satisfaction.

Half of the participants believe that having a positive attitude, combined with consciously choosing positive thoughts and people, adds to their feelings of happiness and empowerment as a woman.

The majority of participants said that completing personal life assessments helps women increase their feelings of empowerment and happiness. All of the participants agreed that women know that greater happiness comes first by choosing a happy marriage and children, then being financially stable, and, finally, having an interesting career. Indeed, the majority of participants claimed that having the courage to choose opportunities aligned with their passions was imperative to women's empowerment and happiness. Thus, the research suggests that improved quality relationships enhances well-being, whereas women mentoring and supporting other women leads to the sharing of insights and the continuation of women's empowerment. The majority of the participants felt that giving back to the community lays the groundwork for a world whose greatest resource is its citizens.

When asked "What would make you feel more empowered/happy/balanced?" the participants said they wanted to do a better job of taking care of themselves, assessing and pursuing personal interests, encouraging life balance, spending quality time with family and friends, and making a positive contribution to the community and the world.

In response to the interview question, "Please list positive qualities of being a woman and positive qualities of being a man, which if combined could benefit society," the majority of participants endorsed the theme that focusing on integration of feminine and masculine energies contributes to happiness and empowerment.

In one of the questions, the participants, who self-assessed themselves as feminine women action-oriented, claimed to have high levels of happiness while feeling frequent stress. On the other hand, the participants reporting as masculine action-oriented felt high and medium levels of happiness while they also felt stress "frequently" and "sometimes." The feminine action-oriented women that moved between combining feminine and masculine aspects at home while relying on their masculine attributes at work rated medium high levels of happiness and frequent stress. There was no participant who self-reported as equally feminine and masculine in all situations. Yet, the majority of participants observed this as the ideal, which would positively enhance an individual's well-being. One of the interesting outcomes shows that most women in this study, although empowered, suffer from frequent stress. This is an aspect that we will analyze further in the chapter.

Based on our assessment, the integration of feminine and masculine attributes, in personal and professional environments, reduces stress and contributes to empowering women. Following this idea, a participant claimed that all men and women have the ability to answer the world's problems through "listening to" and "following" their feminine intuition while relying on their masculine attributes to generate a plan to solve issues. The majority of participants asserted that women's intuitive and empathic qualities are beneficial to the world.

Women's Health. The majority of the participants experienced high levels of stress everyday, whereas only a few spoke of experiencing medium and low levels of stress. The frequency of the stress is the issue. In a biologically healthy response to stress, the individual responds to an immediate crisis by choosing either "fight or flight," once the crisis is averted the individual returns to their normal state. The duration of the stress is important. Biologically, the body responds to stress through raising blood pressure for energy and temporarily turning off the body's nonessential systems, such as tissue repair and reproduction. The impact of stress over extended periods of time on body functions is key in relation to the participants' self-reports of continuous levels of stress. The health issue that derives from the participant's stress is due to multitasking, overburdened schedules, worries, and anxiety. Stress physiologist Hans Selye explains that "the stress-response can be mobilized not only in response to physical or psychological insults, but also in expectation of them. It is this generality of the stress-response that is the most surprising – a physiological system activated not only by all sorts of physical disasters but by just thinking about them as well" (Sapolsky, 2004, p. 7). Recent studies link stress to weight gain, depression, increased blood pressure, clogged arteries leading to heart attacks, and chronic and severe acute stress leads to killing brain cells and breaking apart chromosomes.

Specifically, stress has lingering effects on women. *The Dutch Hunger Winter* study reported that stress in utero affects individuals their entire lifetime. The study followed individuals who were fetuses in the womb when their mother experienced stress during pregnancy. These individuals, even 60 years later, experienced poorer health, cardiovascular disease, lessoned brain capacity, maladaptivity to stress, and vulnerability to psychiatric disorders (Sapolsky, 2004). The Whithall study evaluated British civil servants and concluded that the participants' position in the social hierarchy related directly to their levels of stress. Those individuals in subordinate positions who feel less empowered are more susceptible to heart disease and other diseases (Sapolsky, 2004). For instance, those at the top experienced lower stress, and the stress increased incrementally as positions were farther from the top. Similarly, Sapolsky's Primate study discovered that dominant baboons had low stress and submissive baboons had higher stress due to always being on guard and vigilant. The females had more vulnerable reproductive systems and higher blood pressure. *The Dutch Hunger Winter*, Whithall and Primate studies are valuable when evaluating the contributing factors to a woman's empowerment and relating to the participants' high levels of stress.

As previously noted, each of the participants conveyed stress feelings related either to control or to the lack of control in their lives. Attempting to control experiences is a human act with the intention of inducing good feelings. "Being effective – changing things, influencing things, making things happen – is one of the fundamental needs with which our brains seem to be naturally endowed, and much of our behavior from infancy onward is simply an expression of this penchant for control" (Gilbert, 2006, p. 22). From youth, humans exert specific behaviors to elicit a desired response from each situation. Exercising this right is normal, yet psychological malady for the individuals lies where control is impossible or where they are unable to influence their environment. "Research suggests that if they lose their ability to control things at any point between their entrance and their exit, they become unhappy, helpless, hopeless, and depressed" (Gilbert, 2006, p. 22). To demonstrate this point, in two separate research studies involving the elderly at nursing homes, researchers, respectively, had a high-control and low-control group. In the first study, the high-control group had responsibility for a household plant, while the low-control group a separate individual was assigned to the plant. In the second study, the high-control group set the schedule for visitations, while in the low-control group the visitor set the schedule. In both studies, the low-control group had a higher mortality rate and the high-control group experienced a higher degree of positive attitudes and wellbeing (Gilbert, 2006). As demonstrated, both control groups responded to the study's expectations based on the individual's perceived level of control. The psychological health of the individuals was affected by the perception of their ability to control or not control their life. An individual believing that the uncontrollable is controllable positively influences the impact of the experience, even though the impression of control is an illusion. "In fact, the one group of people who seem generally immune to this illusion are the clinically depressed, who tend to estimate accurately the degree to which they can control events in most situations. These and other findings have led some researchers to conclude that the feelings of control – whether real or illusory – is one of the wellsprings of mental health" (Gilbert, 2006, p. 24). The importance the participants place on their perceived level of control over their life experiences is a key factor.

Research suggests that the traits of the Superwoman Complex are especially vexing for a woman. In the book, *Unleash the Power of the Female Brain*, neuropsychiatrist Daniel Amen conveys,

> As a woman, you face some unique additional challenges. You are far more likely than a man to suffer from anxiety and depression and, in some studies, Alzheimer's disease. You are far more susceptible to recurring negative thoughts you just can't dismiss, to body image struggles that all too frequently morph into eating disorders, and to excessive self-criticism for not being perfect. You are also more prone to pouring yourself into the care of your loved ones and the demands of your job, your family, and your community, finding it ever more difficult to take the time you need to care for yourself. (2013, p. xii)

Amen states that women's brains are prone toward negative thinking, self-criticism, and perfectionism, magnifying flaws and minimizing the good. Women's anxiety of imagined low performance in society is a misconception that causes extreme harm. Regardless, despite Amen's deterministic views on women, we have to accept women are more prone to stress. These neurological vulnerabilities specific to women due to stress are aggravated by the responsibilities they have incurred in the 21st century. An overreliance on material and physical gains in tension with women's innate sensitivities causes a culture of individuals living in basic survival mode without the time and energy to spend on existential needs and requirements.

Indeed, reports show that women experience intense pressure to perform, especially when providing the basic needs of their family. One of the outcomes of the post-recession period in the United States is that many men's workplace roles have downsized while traditional women's roles have become more prevalent. Professor of Organizational Behavior at Michigan Technological University Sonia Goltz notes that within her family, "all the men were out of work and all the women were working. The men were having lots of time to go fishing and hunting, and we're feeling really overworked and stressed" (Mundy, 2012, p. 241).

With these increasing responsibilities, many women are becoming the sole breadwinners, either by managing single parent households or contributing financially. Studies such as those by Mundy (2012) depict women in these roles as having mixed feelings, ranging from pride to resentment. The participants described a common theme of financial obligations restricting their desires. It translates as "Why do I have to be the guy?" (p. 89) A clear expression of the reluctance women felt concerning being a full-time provider on a permanent basis. "They could entertain the idea of earning somewhat more, but did not aspire to be the sole earner" (p. 73). Economically, women were open to temporarily doing so, sharing, or taking turns being the provider, yet accepted the permanent role grudgingly.

Attaining success in a masculine dominated workforce places women at a disadvantage. Professionally women endure continuous pressure in the attempt to live up to unequal expectations. When stacking women against men the studies reflect that men have skills that influence their success, while women's successes are transitory. For men, mistakes are seen as transitory, but when women make mistakes, their competence is placed in question. In turn, a woman is judged harshly against her male peers when she is nearly exemplary, yet not perfect. A woman's actual accomplishments are rated against men's perceived potential (Williams, 2010). Consistently, social science studies confirm that women's overall performance is constantly being evaluated, this requires women to out-perform and extend themselves. As Williams noted, senior male executives "freely admitted that women in upper level positions were subject to competency testing much more often than their male counterparts. Successful women "counter the 'competency barrier'" by "deliver[ing] more than people expect" (p. 94). By most accounts, women are under the microscope, working twice as hard and experiencing extra pressure compared to their male counterparts.

Women who have foregone or delayed having children feel they paid a high price. Many women ask themselves if it is possible to have a career and become a mother. An interesting study explored the relationship between career and children for baby-boomer college-educated women. Of the research population, half the women stated they wanted children. By their late 30s and 40s, less than 20% had both a career and children (Crittenden, 2010). Similarly, Catalyst performed a study of men and women with MBAs. Of these 1,600 individuals, 70% of the men and only one-fifth of the women had children (Crittenden, 2010). These are critical facts when considering the steady increase of women entering the workforce and the impact on maternity, including delaying pregnancy and the later possibility of incurring fertility issues. The ability to achieve and maintain both a professional life and motherhood is a component that ties into survival mode for women. Thus, reinforcing the stress in their lives.

In the opposite spectrum, women with families state that they felt like they had two full-time positions. Hochschild's research "documented how the women she interviewed faced the equivalent of a second job when they returned to the home after work... further shackled them to endless hours of drudgery, to the point of exhaustion" (Bianchi, Robinson, & Milkie, 2006, p. 113).

An interesting aspect to take account is that, within the women who have families, they experience numerous counterproductive feelings, including guilt, imagining they are not doing enough. In the study case referenced by Liza Mundy, a husband spoke of his full-time working wife: "She carries a lot of guilt. . . . I don't really have any guilt" (2012, p. 236). The maternal instinct in a woman deftly defies her ability to love herself and places her in emotional servitude. Succinctly, Balzac quoted, "Maternal love makes of every woman a slave" (Crittenden, 2010, p. 8). Studies demonstrate that working mothers juggling career and household, essentially two full-time positions, fear they are not good mothers. These women are "facing daily challenges and abiding fears that they were being a 'bad mom'" (Williams,

2010, p. 91). It follows that working mothers feel they are not doing well in any one of the roles they perform.

Confounding the emotional impacts, a working mother's schedule is nonstop and rarely involves rest. This prohibits the woman from paying attention to her own needs. Studies have confirmed that working mothers spend over eighty hours a week between their professions and family, sleeping between three to six hours (Crittenden, 2010). One mother stated, "I can't go on; I'm absolutely exhausted," she said. "I'm 43, the kids are in good shape, and I need some rest" (p. 21).

Contrary to the common belief, the fact that women joined the workforce does not reflect negatively on the wellbeing of the children. Today more time is being spent with the children than in the past. In the 21st century, families partake in a form of child rearing that involves *pressure on performance*, which Williams (2010) defines as "intensive mothering." Sharon Hays describes this method as "child-centered, expert-guided, emotional absorbing, labor intensive, and financially expensive" (cit. in Williams, 2010, p. 23). This form of parenting, which originates in parental anxiety, absorbs time and energy, sacrificing other equally important aspects of parents' lives. Lacking true quality time (Bianchi, Robinson, & Milkie, 2006), parents continuously find themselves running from activity to activity in an attempt to expand their children's minds and to prepare them for an uncertain future. The book *Perfect Madness: Motherhood in the Age of Anxiety* describes mothers as anxiously overscheduling their children, making life challenging for themselves in the process, all in an attempt to care for their children (Williams, 2010). A study by Gary Ramey and Valerie A. Ramey agrees that this kind of child rearing exemplifies the parents' drive to create an "after school resume" in our culture's "winner take all economy" and "stems not from children's needs but from parents' anxieties" (Williams, 2010, p. 24). Annette Lareau's class-based book, Unequal Childhoods, describes the fast paced family activities, which leads "everyone – including ten-year-old children – [...] exhausted" (Williams, 2010, p. 166).

The National Survey of Parents' data reports that 71% of married women, 75% of employed women, and 78% of single mothers feel they have too little time for themselves, compared to 57% of fathers, who are more likely to ask for free time that does not involve children (Bianchi, Robinson, & Milkie,

2006). Accordingly, Bianchi reports, mothers have the tendency to sacrifice their needs on behalf of the family and single mothers feel the greatest strain that they are not doing enough, making sacrifices both at home and work.

Startlingly, studies show that employed women have 15 hours less weekly of discretionary, free or leisure time. The opportunity for woman to rest and rejuvenate lacks quality as it often includes their children. This lack of time for relaxation affects women's overall health (Bianchi, Robinson, & Milkie, 2006). "Rather than leisurely, time with children [it] is often hectic and rushed" (p. 129). This is due to the "highly pressured and sped-up version of childhood – and motherhood" (Williams, 2010, p. 3), a hallmark of the degradation of the ability of women to maintain balance in their lives.

Another keynote is the significant impact that the family's schedules have upon the relationship between the parents as a couple. The family's emphasis on the children places the wellbeing of the couple behind children and paid work (Williams, 2010). Between 1975 and 2000, a study evaluating couples saw a dramatic 26% drop in the amount of time couples spend in each other's company. Defining further, employed mothers correlates to 6 hours less a week compared to unemployed mothers. In self-reports from parents, 66% of women and 58% of men felt they wanted to spend more time with their significant other (Bianchi, Robinson, & Milkie, 2006). In addition, low-income families often require one parent working the night shift with the other working the day shift to accommodate their family needs. This results in "everyone ends up exhausted, and many parents rarely see each other awake" (Williams, 2010, p. 4). In interviews by Arlie Hochschild, she "chronicled the long work days of mothers and the resulting strains in their relationships with their husbands" (Bianchi, Robinson, & Milkie, 2006, p. 113).

Other important relationships also are affected by the lack of quality time. Studies suggest that women spend less time "visiting friends and relatives' homes" and that there is a "decline in community involvement" (Bianchi, Robinson, & Milkie, 2006, p. 96). As regards to positive influences, the majority of participants said that spending more time with family and friends would increase their level of happiness.

In essence, the 21st century woman is in a crisis of the soul. All of the elements that affect today's woman extrapolate to the research participants, this can be shown in the participant's feelings of stress and of being overwhelmed; none of them were actively pursuing their dreams. The cultural expectations placed on women identify them as martyrs who can be sacrificed as lambs. This places them into survival mode acting out of fear and anxiety.

Maslow speaks of a cultural disease of "mild and chronic psychopathology and fearfulness," (2011, p. 61) a survival-based affliction, a malady of the mind, a fear of oblivion, even in the face of culturally accepted status symbols.

What is needed is love.

Fear is the opposite of love and has taken hold of Western society. Unconsciously, women are both prisoners and wardens of ego created cells, which physically derives from the illusion of power and control. For women, "fear and doubt are the main attraction of their attention and focus" (Becker, 2007, p. 8). An emphasis on the outer versus inner life leaves women in a reactive mode filled with fear rooted in self-doubt. It promotes a lack of feeling safe, exhibiting scarcity mentalities, guilt ridden, and dealing with "basic survival issues, family and job decisions, personal concerns, and a wealth of retained emotional baggage" (p. 155).

Accordingly, individuals feel vitality-sapping emptiness and daily pressure to live the dream while maintaining a false representation of life. It is exhibited through a reliance on food and substances, compulsive spending, safe jobs over purposeful careers, negative thoughts, family conflicts, feeling tired, compulsive or rejecting of love, people pleasing, and loss of zest for life tied back to the search for external sources of nourishment, containment, and safety (Shimoff, 2010).

Critical to humanity, science has shown that fear induces diseases (dis-ease) and that love enhances health. The Institute of HeartMath cited that five minutes of fear and stress resulted in six hours of decreased immune functioning increasing the participants' vulnerability to parasites, bacteria, and viruses. While studying the impact of love and compassion on body functions, the researchers show a steady increase in IgA, an immune system boosting agent that protects the body from sickness (Shimoff, 2010). This demonstrates that individuals have the capacity to both create illness and heal their bodies. Thus, in each moment we have the decision whether to choose either fear or love, as Shimoff shows:

Love and fear are mutually exclusive energies. Either we're functioning from love, or we're functioning from fear. If we're running our fear programs – worry, anxiety, nervousness – love is essentially off-line. Fear expresses itself physically and mentally as a tightening, limiting force. It sends us into survival mode, or fight or flight, which causes our brain to shut down its normal functioning and direct more energy toward self-protection. Our whole system gets depleted from constantly defending itself. (p. 65)

Imagine for a moment, the 21st century Western woman residing daily in feelings of stress, overwhelming hectic schedules, filled with guilt, feeling unworthy, and gradually building up and storing toxic levels of cortisol and norepinephrine, the stress neurochemicals in their body. This is due to being on constant alert and creating quite literally a fear body, decreasing their health and overall functioning emotionally, physically, spiritually, and intellectually (Shimoff, 2010). Thus, it is critical to humanity for women to identify the sources of their *dis-ease*. This process includes making an active commitment to engage in activities that enhance their wellbeing through proactively finding ways to demonstrate love for themselves, and, thus, allowing a gentle response to life.

Embracing love allows women to immerse into their inner wholeness, enabling them to move away from fear created by external stimuli, and allowing them to feel the peace that comes with trusting their true inner compass.

"We are recalling our divinity" when we choose to act from an unconditional state of love with ourselves, others, and the world (Becker, 2007, p. 11). In Maslow's pyramid, the self-actualizers and transcenders share a consistent trait that is depicted by a "total wholehearted and unconflicted love, acceptance, expressiveness, rather than the more usual mixture of love and hate that passes for love or friendship or sexuality or authority or power" (2011, p. 283). Different from romantic or sexual love, unconditional love activates different areas of the brain such as the superior parietal lobe, right caudate nucleus and insula, as identified in brain scans discovered by researchers of the University of Montreal (Shimoff, 2010). This higher form of love is a state of pure being that elicits peace internally and externally, requiring openness and vulnerability to feelings of affection and acceptance. To be unconditional is to be unlimited. This means no strings attached, no stipulations, and no expectations. Simply stated; unconditional love is an unlimited way of being" (Becker, 2007, p. 15).

Unconditional love must originate with the self in order for a woman to be there for her numerous responsibilities ranging from family, to career, to attaining the life of her dreams. A woman's highest obligation is to love herself without condition, in the manner one would love a child or one's best friend. Ideally, a woman learns to view with positive regard both the inner child, who requires unlimited love and nurturing to grow, and the inner best friend, who deserves support and comforting. In the book *How to Be Your Own Best Friend*, psychologist Mildred Newman claims that individuals should treat themselves with the love and care they would bestow on a living child or a best friend. Similar to knowing when a child is upset and hurt, an individual begins to recognize within herself/himself when they need love, attention, rest, and when to push and when not to push (Newman & Berkowitz, 1971). As one's guardian, "you can respect yourself, admire yourself, take tender care of yourself, reward yourself, feel virtuous, loveworthy, respectworthy" (Maslow, 2011, p. 302). Yet, the type of unconditional support women offer to the world, derives from a sense of self-sacrificing or self-denial, based on their expected duties, not from self-love. "It is feeding the part of you that feels worthless." Several of the participants said they had made sacrifices so that their children would have a better life. There is an ongoing trend of "mothers feeling more of a need to put children and family first as they sacrifice their own need" (Bianchi, Robinson, & Milkie, 2006, p. 141). "The truth is to love yourself with the same intensity you would use to pull yourself up if you were hanging off a cliff with your fingertips. As if your life depended upon it" (Ravikant, 2012, p. 5).

The Director of the Greater Good Science Center and University of California, Berkeley psychology professor Dr. Dacher Keltner claims, "Compassion and benevolence are...rooted in our brain and biology, and ready to be cultivated" (Shimoff, 2010, p. 32). Granted human beings are pre-wired for unconditional love, yet the process still involves challenges requiring gentleness, patience, and building trust, within ourselves (Becker,

2007). Although, individuals innately unconditionally love, they need to train their abilities not to lose them.

Maslow described his notion of self-actualization as being similar to Fromm's "healthy selfishness," where there is a balance between being extremely selfish and unselfish (Maslow, 2011, p. 109). Deeply nurturing the self is an individual's duty prior to extending any care to others.

Numerous research studies support the beneficial health impacts of unconditional love directed toward others. Stephen G. Post, the author of *Why Good Things Happen to Good People*, says, "It's neurologically impossible to be engaged in outward acts of loving kindness and also be experiencing a state of high stress or negativity inside. The higher action, loving, cancels out the lower one, fearing" (Shimoff, 2010, p. 65).

By generating empathy for others, those with whom you interact realize that they are safe from expectations, judgments, hurt, rejection, and the pressure of meeting another's unresolved demands. The lack of conflict, jealousy, and competition loosens the tensions, encouraging the others to relax, treat themselves better, be authentic and vulnerable, feel true intimacy, and pay it forward (Newman & Berkowitz, 1971). Thus acceptance without limits or conditions enhances the quality of all relationships, providing opportunities for altruism and service. "Enlightenment is the pursuit and recognition of light within ourselves. This light, being love, is the active use of our own ability to share the highest qualities of life with each other" (Becker, 2007, p. 60).

Maslow believed that all individuals have "a pressure toward unity of personality" (2011, p. 120). Specifically, this is one area where all the participants agreed. In the research study, each participant readily stated that the ideal individual is a combination of feminine and masculine qualities. Maslow expanded this idea in noting that his self-actualizers resolve dichotomies between head and heart and masculine and feminine, through integration and unity, healing a split within the individual. The goal of the individual is to strive toward wholeness, removing all polarities, enabling the individual to end internal struggles and opening themselves to an abundant universe.

As Newman succinctly expressed, "if we want to become all that is in us to become, we have to use everything we've got – our feelings, our intuition, our intelligence, and our will power – our whole self. If we do, the payoff is enormous" (Newman & Berkowitz, 1971, p. 45).

In terms of psychological health, meditation research confirms that when subjects reach a state of "nonduality" or oneness, the functioning of the brain's right and left hemispheres performed harmoniously and connected (Shimoff, 2010). In a similar study, as Newberg reported, spiritual practices, including meditation and prayer, when focused on wholeness, decreased the "stress and anxiety, increased compassion and empathy, and improved mental clarity" (in Shimoff, 2010, p. 256).

The majority of the participants in our study expressed the importance of integrating new daily strategies for self-reflection, to further understand themselves to increase balance, happiness, and empowerment in their lives. Thus, the participants showed a special awareness towards their desire to find their true selves (Becker, 2007). This aligns with Maslow highly rating individuals, who pay attention to their inner voices and inner world, gaining self-understanding of their moods and needs, philosophically and spiritually.

Maslow believed that "Freud's greatest discovery is that the great cause of much psychological illness is the fear of knowledge of oneself – of one's emotions, impulses, memories, capacities, potentialities, of one's destiny" (2011, p. 54). This psychological illness is derived from both a fear of an individual's inner world and a fear of the outer world, as these are related. Without access to inner motivations, the individual impulsively acts out in the outside world with different degrees of neurotic tendencies (Maslow, 2011). When an individual is unaware of her/his inner life, the contents of the unconscious projects itself onto the external world, thus, creating a disturbance in the self.

The fear of plumbing the depths of the unconscious results in a split of the personality, creating catastrophic effects,

> For these depths are also the source of all his joys, his ability to play, to love, to laugh, and, most important for us, to be creative. By protecting himself against the hell within himself, he also cuts himself off from the heaven within. In the extreme instance, we have the obsessional person, flat, right, rigid, frozen, controlled, cautious, who can't laugh or play or love, or be silly or trusting or childish.

His imagination, his intuitions, his softness, his emotionality tends to be strangulated or distorted. (Maslow, 2011, p. 111)

Individuals have a choice to remain unconscious, stifling their life, stagnating in fear. Though, this choice creates neurotic impulses that threaten their perfect mirage causing disorder. Yet, to awaken and say yes to life and to themselves means living the life they are truly meant to live, an intrinsic whole being.

The journey toward self-actualization is a process that is ongoing; in each moment the individual may choose the regressive retracting fear stance or the progressive opening love stance, representing the individual's full potentiality and possibilities (Maslow, 2011). The former option involves much energy to maintain as it is a split of the personality. This split causes the individual to live in disharmony through suppressing/repressing their authentic humanness. The latter option asks from the individual courage, honesty, and the responsibility to take continued right action in alignment with their inner desires and needs. As "one cannot choose wisely for a life unless he dares to listen to himself, his own self, at each moment in life" (Maslow, 2011, pp. 45-46). Consciously, each time individuals make choices honoring their inner world, the decisions positively reflect in their outer world, mirroring what truly makes the individuals happy and empowered, from the deepest recesses of their soul.

Having it All. The significance of finding women living in survival mode critically alters the images associated with "living the American dream" and "having it all." A fearful woman correlates to a fearful society and vice versa, with far-reaching impacts yet to be fully understood. In our research findings, there were an overwhelming number of references associated with women living in survival mode and fear. For example, one participant said, "women are pulled in so many directions and there's an automatic guilt complex that they're trying to balance work and family. They're trying to do it all because they assume they need to be good in every single role that they hold." Particularly, another participant said:

> Do you remember that [1980 Enjoli perfume] commercial bring home the bacon, fry it up in a pan, and still never let him forget he's a man? I think that today women are taking on what [have been] traditionally more

male roles. We had a woman run for presidency. We've got the large paradigm shift in a lot of different areas where women are bringing home, maybe they're making more of the financial money and the husband is staying home with the kids. If you're educated, if you're achieving the goals that you've set for yourself, then hopefully you are doing that for the betterment of yourself and happiness for yourself and others. If they are doing it out of survival, right, you are single mother. I think that marriages are not as prominent, as long-term marriages. They get married, they have kids, and then they get divorced. Higher now, so you have a lot of single women. The males are losing jobs and the females are bringing the monies home. Maybe they want to stay home with the babies and not have to have that role of the financial burden. Taking them out of the traditional women expectation, or things that people used to think that women were and maybe they have the desire to have those things. Maybe they come up from a nuclear family growing up, maybe they are thinking, gosh I thought that I was going to be married and have kids and stay at home. Now I'm divorced, have kids, I'm trying to make the money.

Women living out of a defensive structure place a tremendous burden on themselves, relationships, and families. As women secure professional and financial gains, they acquire economic stability, and families prosper. When these are accessed through a defensive anxious function, it negatively impacts the individual, thus affecting their relationships. For instance, couples' issues surrounding men's "identity, and power, and self-worth" surface, with relational arguments, decreases in happiness, and increases in affairs and divorces as women out-earn men, reported in research in Finland, Germany, and United States by sociologist Jay Teachman in 2010 (Mundy, 2012, p. 89). A participant said that "spending more time with my kids in a non-stressed environment," meaning not running from activity to activity, would make her happy the rest of her life. A participant said:

[In] the 1950's role, the woman was to keep the house clean, make sure the meals are cooked, make sure the house is taken care of. Now in the 2000s women are looked at to be in business and having a career and being able to balance the two. Men aren't taking the role within the household and saying let me wash clothes for you, or let me clean the bathroom on Saturday. Women are still expected to do that, take care of the children, do all the household stuff, and have a career. To do both, you have zero time for yourself. Men it's considered normal, for after work they get to go out and have a drink with the guys because they're still working. If a woman does that then the kids are being neglected or the house is being neglected or somebody didn't go to the grocery store. It's a catch-22 these days because if you're a man applying for a position and you have children you are looked at different. If you're a woman with children, applying for the same position your looked at like, oh my gosh, she's got to leave early to go pick them up from school. The perception is there, that the woman is somehow responsible for everything in the house and children and the man is the backup.

Women experience the impact of various aspects out of their control. The new dynamics of economics has not been readjusted within the walls of the household, adding additional stress to women. A participant said concerning her relationship, its "kind of been out of whack because he's been out of work for over ten years. It wasn't ten years, it was like eight years and so he just got back in the saddle in the last year." A participant said she felt stress by "things in life that you can't control, family, health of the family, their unemployment or employment. How that impacts you." Additionally, a participant said:

> Women's responsibilities and education, and professional lives have evolved and developed. We're definitely a dominant group in the workforce, but unfortunately we haven't offloaded any of the traditionally female roles as mother, caregiver, family organizer. We've

taken on two jobs instead of one job. Before we could defer to the husband for discipline and for financial matters. Now we're just as responsible as they are plus we have a list of things that men would never consider dealing with. We've got two jobs, full-time jobs. Basically [that] means there's less time for personal de-stressing, relaxation, or pursuit of spiritual matters. You don't fill the tank back up.

The continuing pressure that women face in today's society leads women to respond to the challenges through survival mode. This survival mode is associated with the health degradation of women, in particular its implications to long-term stress. The majority of participants said they felt stress frequently and all felt they were overfunctioning and overburdened in their lives. In the following, participants shared their thoughts concerning stress. Although the poll is anonymous, we are going to assign a random number to each individual to avoid possible confusion between transcripts.

- Participant #1: Stress "frequently…. Rather handling fire after fire after fire. Trying to get all the other stuff done somehow as well. Adds a lot of stress. The other things that adds stress is family and health and finances that go hand in hand with the family as a whole."

- Participant #2: "Stress, frequently. Stress is just a fact of life, I have it on a daily basis. Definitely, stress on a daily basis…. I've got so many balls in the air. I work hard to manage it."

- Participant #3: "I have so much to do at work. When you have so much to do for plans and timing, meetings and events with your family and kids. Preparing to go out of town for whether it is work or pleasure."

- Participant #4: Stress "frequently. I would say frequently, I'm always stressed. I put a lot of pressure on myself whether it's my personal life or my professional life. I always want to fix things and do things. I'm highly…..organized. A lot of times I put pressure on myself to get things done. Even before their due, and I put a lot of stress on myself if I don't finish things a certain way. I want to do it right."

- Participant #5: Stress "Frequently. Financial responsibility. Work, personal life balance, being able to fulfill the obligations that I commit to that I should say no to. Too many people want me to do too much and my time is spread thin. Need to take more time, just taking time for me, doing things where I get away and just have some peace and quiet. I haven't done enough of that, taking vacations more things like that."

- Participant #6: "Waking up too early to try to get everything done because there is not enough time in the day. Caring for a family and working full-time (extends) the day beyond what's easy. It eliminates any downtime."

In an effort to reduce stress and set boundaries, half of the participants said, "not very often," when asked how often do you say no? Specifically, a participant said, "Rarely. Interesting point. Interesting that that would be the case. Thought provoking." The participants were asked, what can you do today to increase your level of happiness? Upon reflection, another participant said, "take more time for myself to work some of those things in. Better time management. Asking for the time from people who I'm normally giving to." In response to the question, another participant said:

> Say no more. I am a person who thinks I can do it better than anybody else and usually I can. I end up being put in those positions where I end up taking on too much. That's part of the saying no. That's in being there for my friends, if anybody needs to borrow money, if anybody needs help setting up for a party, if anybody needs ice. At work, it's the project management stuff. I say I take on too much because I firmly don't want to let people down and I think I can do it better than anybody else. I've created that pattern for myself that people always know they can come to me and I don't say no. My biggest thing is pushing back and saying no more to give me time or give me some space.

During the interviews, when the participants were asked why they were not currently pursuing a career that would make them happy for the rest of their life, these participants responded in the following manner:

- Participant #7: "Money. Following a career choice that I really wanted versus one that circumstances led to. I have succeeded and earn a lot of money but [it] doesn't bring the reward that my true passion would bring."

- Participant #8: "There are things there, let's say financial. I am very much into meeting my obligations and being very dependable and all that."

- Participant #9: "Responsibility. I enjoy what I do, but it is also the stress that comes along with it. If I had to picture what is the opposite of what I do today it would be low stress. Have more of a serene type of life without the stress. One of the crazy yoga instructors on a beach somewhere. Just something very low key exactly opposite what I do now. I don't do that because of the responsibilities I carry. I have financial responsibilities on me for my nephew and for my mom, things like that that comes first. My thought process goes to what is going to make everything secure, stable, and nothings crazy is going to happen. No drama."

- Participant #10: "You get on a work path of making money and supporting a lifestyle and to transition into a very different lifestyle takes a lot of planning and leaps of faith and time that its hard to get off the treadmill."

Women in today's society are impacted by the benefits and impediments of capitalism. These benefits are expressed through material gains in the United States, yet the citizens live in fear and are restricted by obligations. Easily, the United States is one of the wealthiest countries in the world. Yet, there is a distinct gap between the wealthy and the working poor, whereas the former attempts to grow and maintain their wealth, the latter works to survive. In both communities, the levels of depression, anxiety, unhappiness and stress related diseases are markedly high. With this said, are the United States' principles and values growth inhibiting or growth fostering for the psychological health of its citizens? The answer appears clear.

Notably, the country of Bhutan reformed its politics to include Gross National Happiness. Bhutan measures the happiness of its citizens as a reflection of the highest values of its country. How are the United States' values both propelling and impeding its citizens? Case in point, the principles in which the United States stands for such as democracy and capitalism propels its citizens, yet an overreliance on capitalism impedes its citizens from reaching the ultimate goal in life, happiness. The ideal balance is the easy differentiation between ends (tranquility, serenity, peace) and means (money, power, status)" (Maslow, 2011, p. 122).

Time magazine conducted a poll and the results stated women are more educated, more powerful than ever before, but are less happy – why do you feel the women polled felt this way? A participant shared,

> Women, more than ever before, always try to do too much. I think that a lot of times that you focus on all those things instead of some of the things that you really are passionate about. Whether it's your family or sports activities or book clubs or whatever it is. I think women many times throw themselves into all those things and forget about who they are versus trying to live their life. I imagine that's why they are less happy because they are just not giving enough time to themselves.

Corroborating, another participant said, "Certain women that are unhappy that they didn't do the things they want out of life. That they didn't stop [to] smell the roses, shall we say."

An important question we want to answer was whether the participants endorsed Jung's theories concerning balancing the masculine and feminine. In a world of dichotomies, the findings identified masculine and feminine energies within an individual are not mutually exclusive, and their transcendence consummates a higher unified experience (Maslow, 2011). Essentially, "neither masculinity nor femininity, as conventionally defined, is a recipe for a centered life" (Williams, 2010, p. 104) thus evolving into a balanced individual necessitates integration.

Rather than polarizing one or the other and expressing extremes in personality, each participant agreed that the balanced individual was a combination of masculine and feminine attributes. The participants were asked to list the positive qualities of being a woman and the positive qualities of being a man, and to explain what combined qualities could benefit society. In response, one participant expressed that the ideal individual is the one who intuits what is needed through their feminine function and takes action through their masculine nature to benefit society. For example, a participant articulated that women have the,

Ability to follow intuition and trust intuition. I think that that alone would be a big help to society. I think we all have inside of us the ability to answer the world's problems if we listen to ourselves and communicate what we feel is the right thing to do, and then from a masculine perspective generate a plan to create action that solves issues. Following intuition more and trusting your gut when something appears to be wrong to follow through and do something to make it right.

Similarly, another participant said the "blended ideal person has a strength, but does not automatically assume that, more empathic, not as focused on power as they are in doing the right thing." In each instance, the participants emphasize the importance of doing the right thing through intuiting (feminine) the right use of strength (masculine). As a result, it is only the union of these two principles that constitutes a complete human being. This conclusion relates to other theorists, such as Sanford who shares "their union is realized in every man and every woman within their bisexual, androgynous nature, and it also takes place through the intercommunication between the two natures, the masculine and the feminine." (Sanford, 1980, p. 6). It is necessary to combine the masculine and feminine, yet we have to be conscious that the union and duality is not based on sexual tendencies, but specific to masculine and feminine character traits. Following with this thought, a participant said,

I wonder how many of those things [characteristics] we absolutely have to have that's strictly masculine. That's the tough thing because women have taken on so many roles of men now that they are no longer masculine, any more masculine than they are feminine.... Most women in business are a combination of masculine and feminine today. Where they have the confidence and the ability to be outspoken and communicate their ideas. Feeling that their ideas are as important as anybody else's.

Additionally, another participant said:

> Male and female, I don't see a whole lot of. There's
> qualities that would be for both. The male and the female
> qualities almost run together for me personally. I've seen
> them in both. Really, I don't see a whole lot of division
> between male and female, truly. I don't see a whole
> lot of difference in the two genders. My stance is that
> they are combined. They kind of combine for me. The
> attributes between a male and a female or we'll call it a
> "neutral gender" because truly its creativity from a male
> or female standpoint, its creativity, its caring, and sharing
> and growing other individuals as well as themselves. It's
> making this world as positive for themselves so that they
> can make it positive for others in a larger perspective.
> Using your talents to get out and leverage them in maybe
> not just one-on-one but to the larger side of the world.

We can acknowledge how the participants made an effort to make the
unconscious conscious. An important aspect is that to truly identify their
needs self-reflection is pivotal to these women. As another participant said,
"Spend more time assessing how I spend my days and what I'm thinking
and what I'm doing. To make sure that the things that are getting missed get
added back in to be more balanced. Might add to empowerment and having
a healthier balance. Something that seemed obvious to myself while I was
answering those questions. Let's see if I can play that off."

All of the participants agreed that women are responsible for their
own happiness and have the ability to make their own destiny. As one
participant said:

> This is what I completely believe in. That you have
> to live the life that you want to live. You can't depend
> on others to make you happy. I say this because I tell my
> sister and my family and some of my friends, this too, is
> that because they complain all the time about certain
> things. You know, what if that's the case then change it. I
> believe that you can do things. You can't sit around and
> wait for other people to make you happy. If you want

certain things, certain things are going to fulfill you. Go to school, or take a class, join a gym, do whatever you want. Go travel, visit a new country, meet new people. You have to do it. You have to go out and put yourself out there and do it. I completely believe in that. So you have to make your own destiny. Ultimately, happiness comes from there, because you feel fulfilled. The glass is always half full for me. I really believe life is too short. Grab the chance. Take it. You have an opportunity to do something that you want to do and find happiness. Just don't sit and complain. Just do it. So simple. That's the message I want to convey to my children. Although my son would tell you that he has a hard life, you know. He's so stressed because he has homework, has school, and he has soccer. A lot of people ask, "Are you really happy?" "Well yea, what's there not to be happy about?"

During the interviews, all of the participants articulated that women sacrifice in order to provide their children a better life, depriving themselves of their heart's desires to fulfill the need for their child (Bianchi, Robinson, & Milkie, 2006). Some of the participants stated that women should have the same expectations for themselves as the ones they expect for their children. Continuing this theme, a participant said that she would like to "see a women that is actually trying to do for herself what she wished for her children."

The majority of the participants agreed that the ultimate happiness is to focus, in order of importance, on having happy relationships, children if they choose to have children, being financially stable, and an interesting career they are passionate about. In the *Time* magazine poll, women rated various words in order of importance for themselves and the results were as follows: (1) Interesting Career, (2) Financial Success, (3) Happy Marriage and Children. When the same women were asked what they would want most for their own daughters, they ranked in order of importance the exact opposite: (1) Happy Marriage and Children, (2) Financial Success, and (3) Interesting Career. We asked the participants, why do you think the women polled wanted something different for themselves than they wanted for their own daughters? A participant said, "They feel they paid a price in order to have the interesting career and financial success. They feel they came at the price of some of their own happiness and the happiness of their children." Another participant said:

> They are wanting better, they think what they have is not the best, it's not the greatest, it's not the thing they've always wanted in life. It's the thing that they have to do, they need to do to survive, to be able to do things that are better for their kids. It's the classic, I want better for my children than I had for myself. That's exactly what they're doing they are surviving and doing what they think that they need to do so that their children can have the better life. They're obviously wanting better, because they think that they're kids would be happier the other way around. If that's the case in their mind then that's what they would believe for themselves as well. They should be wanting that for themselves. But they're not doing it. They're not giving themselves what they are trying to provide for their own children. Which is too bad, that's not a good thing. The better life is truly opposite of how they ranked them. Which is have a happy family, be financially stable, and then have an interesting career.

Another participant said, "I think deep down inside they knew that's what they needed more of." Following this quote, the next participant stated:

> They are ranking, to them, perhaps that having a family and having a happy marriage is perhaps #1, it's what they want for their children. A lot of times you want what's best for your children. You work so that your children can have the things you didn't have when you were in your childhood. I think for the women having that put on first for their daughters is they themselves view that as a critical piece. Because to them having a marriage and children, happy marriage and having children is actually the most important thing. As opposed to list the other piece. They realize being happy is more important than having a career and having money financial reward. They would want that,

we want what's best for our children. We moved to Irvine for our children. For their education, my husband and I. We consciously made our decision to move to Irvine because we wanted the kids to have a good education. A good public school. Irvine is known for that, so we moved here consciously for that. So you want what's best for your children. I think that's the survey. A lot times, you don't put yourself first, right. You think that I gotta do this, I have to do this in order to be successful. But I want a better life for my children. So that's why they chose that. I would choose children and marriage first and then the rest would come in for myself. That to me is the ultimate happiness, because your family comes first and then everything else falls into place. What makes all of us happy. It might not be children, it might just being happy finding somebody you love. Really ultimately, all of us in this world finding that person that your compatible with and you want to share your life with. Some people might not have children and that's ok. Other people. I think as humans, we want this is what we strive for, right. We don't want to be alone.

Agreeing and using similar words, the following participant said:

I think the most difficult thing to do is to have a successful marriage and happy healthy children. Reality sets in that you got to have a successful career and you've got to have financial stability in order to have a happy home life. In a perfect world, you'd have a great husband, and he'd have a great job, and you'd be able to raise beautiful kids in the great big house on the cul-de-sac. But in reality that's not what really happens. They want that for their daughters, whether its reality or not, is a different thing.

Finally, the last participant commented:

I think the thought they wouldn't have a happy marriage or have happy children was too discouraging to them. Where maybe they already felt like they had a happy marriage and happy children. They could push it to the bottom of the list. They took it for granted. Maybe, because they were in pursuit. Maybe the idea of just traditional thinking ingrained in their heads still. You know the role of a woman is to have, you know, be a good mother first before a good career person. Maybe there's just some stereotypes that are hanging out still. They think that maybe they are that there's gonna be a correction at some point where women get back to focusing in on those things. Maybe in our next generation.

Interestingly enough, most of the participants stated that the women in the *Time* magazine poll do not provide for themselves what they want for their children. They all state that women, in order to achieve empowerment, first need to take care of their inner needs. We conclude that women, in general, are sacrificing themselves for the happiness of their children, making them unavailable to attain happiness for themselves.

Relating to the above queries, in the 21st century, new "femme" feminists are "calling for greater opportunities for part-time work and valuing (monetarily) stay-at-home parents" (Williams, 2010, p. 125). Whether a woman chooses to marry, have children, or not, while pursuing a fulfilling career, the United States has a responsibility to assist its citizens in the overreaching theme of "having it all" by offering more flexibility and work options in policies and benefits. Following this theme, a participant said:

> With the women's movement back in the 70's, is that a lot of the time some take it to the extreme where they can't find the balance of it. I mean even now, finding a balance is hard. I feel like there's a lot of stress that we take on ourselves too. Finding the balance that ok, when is it enough? When do I know it is time for work, right, time for my husband, time for my family.... Talking about women who think that they can't have both. They can't have a family and go to work at the same time and be educated at the same time. If they had a goal in mind that sometimes they focused on that so much that then missed their opportunity to say if they wanted to start a family or not. I belong to a group of women, Bunko women that

actually meet once a month. There's only a few working moms in this situation. A lot of them are not working, so they are concentrating on their family. There's a lot less people that I know that are working and having a family, at the same time managing it. Some people are opting to do one or the other. I have single girlfriends who are single and happy with their career. My single women friends, they are quite happy and realize that they did want to have a different life then they have right now. Although, some went to therapy to find that out. Others discovered that they didn't need that so-called traditional value. I've known women that are working women like myself that are happy that's managing it. I can't say that I'm able to do everything, because I can't have activities with the kids or spend time with the kids like the other moms do. I'm ok with that and the kids are well adjusted and their doing good fine. They have enough activities, not too much that we're not in competition with each other. It's a balance, ultimately. It's all about balance.

The eldest of the participants reflects on her life, saying:

If I had to do it all over again, I would do things differently. Not saying that my life had been bad, there's been ups and downs. In the end, I don't feel I've had a rewarding career. I just feel as you get older you learn more of life's passions and what you are truly about and would love to have the opportunity to go pursue those interests and make that the career instead of what I came into by circumstance along the way. I want a do over. Years ago, when I was in school, I started taking architecture and I was so intimidated because I was the only girl in the class and I was so shy at that age and I just, I think after two classes I went down and said I need to change classes. I got out of it and really that is one of my passions and I would love to have been an architect or an interior designer or something along those lines. At that young age, I couldn't control that shyness and intimidation. I just didn't pursue that and I would now, I would. Then, I couldn't and I would have just loved to have gone down that path in life and really focused on that. I think I would have married later, had a family later. Started the career then maybe cut back a little bit and had a family and obviously continued along with it. I think I would have done it differently. I just financially do not feel in a position to do that (now) and risk my retirement years.

The last quote shows how some of the participants selected a similar road to the women in the *Time* magazine poll, choosing financial stability over their and their families' happiness. Yet, the price is acknowledged, as a new trend forges empowered woman who focus on their inner goals. For an individual to determine what she really wants while following that internal guidance is crucial to determining what makes her feel empowered and happy. What is significant in the findings is that:

> It looks as if there were a single ultimate value for mankind, a far goal toward which all men strive. This is called variously by different authors self-actualization, self-realization, integration, psychological health, individuation, autonomy, creativity, productivity, but they all agree that this amounts to realizing the potentialities of the person, that is to say, becoming fully human, everything that the person can become. (Maslow, 2011, p. 118)

The study's intention was to address the question of what unconsciously restricts and what consciously cultivates the participants' potentialities. We determined that unconscious restrictions might be overcome through transcending fear and embracing unconditional love. On the other hand, an individual's potentialities might be achieved by courageously integrating all aspects of the individual.

Far Reaching Influence. The intention is to provide critical themes and insightful material applicable of being a change agent. In particular, there is a distinct tie between women's psychological health and impacts to the world. In various disciplines, women's psychological health is a robustly researched topic, yet, the rates of anxiety and depression continue to escalate.

We have made a unique contribution as the research material is readily available to the therapeutic community as well as women at home suffering alone, transitioning the research from a purely theoretical context to the utilitarian.

Compared to previous research, the narrative "voice" of the women participants differentiates the research, outlining how they feel about their empowerment and happiness. Based on the findings, the key themes are overcoming fear, embracing unconditional love, balancing the masculine and feminine, and inner work leading to self-actualization.

Furthermore, a woman's far-reaching impact should not be underestimated. The details of why women's wellbeing is important are present in this analysis of women's current state of mind. The findings outline the vital steps toward healing for each individual. One example may be seen in the words of the next participant,

> I think I'm missing some things. I think I could spend more time supporting aspirations and less time on busy work that is not my priority. Support my dreams. I think activities supporting dreams or goals, I'd like to see more of those in my daily life.

Reflection on the results of this research leads us to conclude that many women today are experiencing a crisis of the soul, yet they have the self-reflection necessary to restore health. The next step is to implement its restoration.

Specifically, we were struck by the degree to which fear and self-actualization emerged as key themes. For instance, a participant said, "What makes me happiest is what can provide me the stability and security. Not putting myself at risk sometimes because I want that stability. I put those things first....In a bad way, I put my career and my security first sometimes." This was an unanticipated finding. The emphasis on fear is related to the participants' anxiety about outcome, impoverishment, lack of dependability, overburdened responsibilities, and obligations. Living out of fear is an issue that promotes feelings of being stifled, loss of zest of life and aliveness, checking out of life, feeling dead inside, and numb to life. Yet concurrently, the participants demonstrated an unstifled urge to fight against the tide, seeking life-blood and vitality through self-actualization. The interviews highlighted their courage and strength of will to do the inner work necessary to move forward. Echoing these sentiments a participant said:

> It is such an individual experience, it is all what that individual, that person wants, what they're passionate about. I mean what makes you wake up, want to wake up everyday and carry on with the day. What makes me want to wake up and have a great day. Or at the end of the night, when you are sitting around with the family saying, "What did you do that was great? What would you change?" I think it is just always doing a check of yourself every morning and night wondering what you could have done differently to make yourself happy. Also other people happy and who you touched that day and maybe something that came great of it or something you'd do differently next time. If we take the time to invest more in ourselves, I think that I think we'd have a lot more happier people out there versus everybody kinda doing the rat race everyday.

The intention was to explore the pulse of today's woman, and it is clear that women need to learn more ways to love, nourish, and feed the self, pay attention to their feelings, and remain in tune and present each moment to their needs. Much knowledge may be gained through understanding the practices of those women who feel "filled up" by their daily practices.

In relation to her present sense of empowerment, a participant shared, "Moments of spirituality, which in my case happen to be areas of nature like going hiking or backpacking or exposing myself to beautiful things in the outdoors, confidence building and inspiring." Another participant said, "I don't start my day without thanking the higher powers, that I am so blessed to have everything that I have…I have been very blessed. I live a very (good life), things work out for me."

Maslow spoke in depth concerning the connection between peak moments and self-actualization. In the 21st century, where identifying one's vitality and life-blood have the appearance of happening only in the movies and myths, how may following a path of joy and happiness indicators in our daily lives consciously expand our ability to follow our heart's desires? In the findings, we noted the majority of participants did not ask themselves what would bring happiness and joy into their lives. If they are not taking these basic notions of their overall wellbeing into account, then is it not surprising that most individuals' unfulfilled lives do not reflect their true selves.

In terms of peak experiences, the findings identified that half of the participants felt that spending more time with family and friends and taking vacations would increase their levels of empowerment and happiness. One of the participants believes that her happiness would increase if she could have "time to spend with family and friends," and another participant said the happiest time of her life was when she was "able to reconnect with a lot of friends...mainly just spending a lot of time with my friends and family." As stated previously, a participant shared she would like "spending more time with my kids in a non-stressed environment." Vacations was also a key component for one participant, who said, "I like taking vacations and going on adventures...we took a vacation recently just the two of us. Knowing, realizing that we need time as a couple to be with each other without the children." Echoing these sentiments, a participant said, "I take every single day of my vacation that's available." In contrast, another participant said, "I haven't done enough of that, taking vacations more things like that." Additionally, a few of the participants were looking for more serenity in their life. When asked, what would make them happy for the rest of their lives, one of the participants said, "Have more of a serene type of life," and another participant said, "A whole true feeling of contentness. I can't just pin it on one thing. Really being content with everything...kind of always being that content and peaceful."

In the interviews, half of the participants believed gratitude, positive thinking, and surrounding oneself with positive individuals are important to the empowerment of women. A participant shared the character traits of empowered women are "positive thinking, positive living, I always try to believe good in others. Be confident about yourself and what you bring to the table." One component identified in the findings was the importance of spiritual, inspiring, unique thinking friends. A participant explained her life enhancing strategies were "spending more time with family and people that make you feel good. Choosing activities or work that I'm good at. Making choices to be around positive people....I have friends who are deeply spiritual, they're very inspiring. That are unique thinkers." One participant outlined her specific daily practices that contributed to her feelings of empowerment and happiness:

> I love the way I live my life. I am a very positive thinker. I am very grateful and I make sure to express that on a daily basis. Not out loud. It is something very personal. I do it in the shower, right before my feet hit the ground, I am already saying thank you and appreciating the things that aren't even in place. I have mantras that I do, things that I do in the morning, afternoon, and evening that keep me in a positive frame of mind. The positive thought attracts. It's a lot of attraction. Positive and those things that you think about most attract to you.... I try to keep positive thoughts going. Very much a believer in, the biggest thought is where attention goes. When you are thinking about something, when you are thinking about success, you are thinking about the positive things then those are drawn to you. I am a firm believer in the vision and the super mind where you think that your life is one way and it becomes that way. So it's already happened for you. I start doing that early in the morning. I do it whenever is possible. I feel very happy... I am very much into creating a positive atmosphere where, you know, I keep myself in check. I try to surround myself with the right individuals... I try to find the positive and be happy every single day. In some way, even if it is a small manner.

Further research is necessary concerning the conscious ability to continuously choose positive thoughts, individuals, and environments. The more an individual surrounds themselves with positive thoughts, positive individuals and good surroundings the more these situations are attracted into their lives.

The idea of conscious choice was an area the participants agreed upon. Individuals create their lives through critical life assessments, choosing passionate opportunities and realizing that women are responsible for their own happiness. They all agree they have the ability to achieve their own destiny.

The findings provided a greater understanding of the innate knowledge accessible within each participant by excavating through their inner depths. A participant said, "It's good to actually hear myself say these things out loud because it gives me a little bit more assurance and beliefs that I am going toward that next paradigm shift in my life. The next reinvention. I'm happy with the things I heard myself saying."

The participants agreed that women's intuitive and empathic qualities are beneficial to the world. They believe that men and women have the ability to answer the world's problems by listening and following their intuition (feminine) and by generating plans to create actions that solve issues (masculine).

Role models were important in each of the women's lives. These figures were parents, grandparents, friends, and work mentors. At times they provided a model of what not to do.

Participant #11 said:

> One of my first employers who interviewed me and told me I wasn't qualified for the job but liked what he saw and thought I had the ability to do so much more. An individual I dated after first divorce sort of restored my confidence. Just having the drive and thinking that yes, I can do this, and going for it when I would read an article in the paper about an up and coming industry leaping into it and not being afraid to go and try it, and try something new. Being divorced a few times, I learned to stand on my own two feet. It's a lot to do with determination. Being the right place at the right time, meeting the right individuals, being persuasive and seeing an opportunity, recognizing it as such and being able to capitalize on it.

Participant #12 said:

> Education was spurred from my father's saying, "this is something that you pretty much do not want to go throughout life without." He also trusted. I had jobs starting at 15 years old. I lived with my grandparents for I would say 2, 3, 4 years of formative time in my life where

I was molded to who I am today from an empowerment and individual, independent type person, in my early teenage years. Never really had families at the table for dinner. Grandparents' house they did. That kind of gave me confidence. Gave me that base that I always believed that I got the base of my ethics and the goals that I am going for. That was one of the biggest empowerments. (Professionally) Mentor to me early on in my career. It was one of my first interviewed for a position and got it. Having management and or other individuals that allow me to be who I am and use those talents have really given me a strong sense of empowerment.

Participant #13 said:

A lady (mentor) that gave me the opportunity to go up there and really supported me and came to visit me. She provided me a lot of executive coaching and counseling to really understand the way the world, the real world, meant.

Participant #14 said:

Early in my childhood, I came over here to the U.S. as an immigrant. As a boat people, part of the boat people from Vietnam. Didn't know a word of English so that actually having immersed myself in a new culture, new language, new lifestyle changed me completely.

Participant #15 said:

My mother and my father. I was always put in situations where I just had to adapt, quickly. Chin up, deal with it. I always just kind of dealt with it. I didn't wallow in it, I just dealt with it. I've had a negative role model that showed me what I didn't want. I went to the opposite extreme. I didn't really have a good role model, a positive role model. I had the bad examples and how I didn't want to be like that.

Participant #16 said:

> Parents that were very encouraging and supportive
> that made you feel you could do anything and not be
> fearful of anything. Reinforcement of that when things
> were bad there was never any criticism. Problem solving,
> teaching confidence in problem solving. Miscellaneous
> opportunities to succeed, like whether that be in sports
> have little victories to add to the confidence or friendship
> interaction where you've got positive reinforcement, that
> you are nice person, and people like to be around you.
> My mother, definitely, and my dad who is always 100%
> supportive.

The findings concerning the study of women's empowerment,
particularly in correlation to their degree of happiness, are extremely
relevant to society as a whole. The themes of fear-based survival mode versus
love-based unconditional love (or, to put it more simply, fear versus love)
are ones the community needs to take very seriously. The impact of being
caught in a fear-based survival mode is repression, denial, and unhealthy
coping responses from human diminution expressed in "the lost pleasures,
joys, and ecstasies,... the inability to relax, the weakening of will, the fear of
responsibility" and "at the extreme we have the experientially empty person,
the zombie, the one with empty insides" (Maslow, 2011, pp. 32-33).

The theme of unconditional love ties into how individuals learn to feed
and nurture themselves. Individuals need to recognize their defenses, and
over time, through listening to their inner voices, to create a loving friendship
with the self, and then extend this same accepting compassionate feeling
outwards in their interactions with others. These generally recognized truths
were brought to life in the participants' own observations. As a participant
described,

> I think it is just always doing a check of yourself every
> morning and night wondering what you could have done
> differently to make yourself happy. Also other people happy
> and who you touched that day and maybe something that
> came great of it or something you'd do differently next
> time. If we take the time to invest more in ourselves, I think

that I think we'd have a lot more happier people out there versus everybody kinda doing the rat race everyday.

Another participant said that she would like to "see a woman that is actually trying to do for herself that she wished for her children" and she expressed that a character trait of an empowered woman is the,

> Ability to utilize the talents that you've created and grown and fostered and brought to fruition within your own person. Sharing those with others, to be able to help them achieve the things that they want to in life. I believe in supporting other women.

For individuals, the integration of the different parts of themselves is integral to a positive life experience. This encompasses accepting the duality of themselves, meaning integrating the anima within men and the animus within women to achieve the unification of the self. The masculine and feminine attributes that each other offers may be implemented to varying degrees depending on the needs of the individual. The final goal of this process is to avoid the polarization of the extremes and achieve wholeness, the symbolic mandala, whereas oneness and nonduality interchangeably represent the highest states of happiness. This state of mind allows the individual to become his or her own healer.

Part of achieving this state of happiness relates taking an active responsibility in making the unconscious conscious. A participant said that she would like to "spend more time assessing how I spend my days and what I'm thinking and what I'm doing." The findings highlighted how Western living standards discourage self-reflection. Living out of fear-based survival mode, the participants were in a constant state of responding to an endless onslaught of responsibilities and obligations, often times self-imposed.

We conclude fear-based survival mode as the 21st century Western crisis of the soul, one in which the "individual as healer" has the opportunity to intervene. A stalling or stagnation of human potentialities was witnessed to over and over again in the research. Each of the participants cited financial responsibilities as reasons why they were not currently pursuing what would make them happy for the rest of their lives and why many had an overreliance on the animus as a means of protection in today's society. These obligations to live were suffocating their psychological health. An aspect that flourished in the participants by being internally called in a different direction for fulfillment, whether or not they were able to listen and to act upon this call or not. The eldest of the participants shared her regret: "If I had to do it all over again, I would do things differently.... I just feel as you get older you learn more of life's passions and what your truly about and would love to have the opportunity to go pursue those interests.... I want a do over."

They said it was the demands of their daily lives that restricted the paths that their heart was telling them to follow. This conflict leads into a high state of stress, or survival mode. Which in turn affects their psychological and physical health.

The next step to acknowledge the problem is to act. In the following, we are going to enumerate the steps to achieving empowerment, happiness, and wholeness (balance):

- **Step 1 – Unconditional Love**
- **Step 2 – Integrating the Feminine and the Masculine**
- **Step 3 – Making the Unconscious Conscious**

With this said, individuals are unique and approaching these steps may involve different processes that feel comfortable to each individual. Please feel free to pick and choose the activities that feel healing to your "Inner Sage."

- **Step 1 – Unconditional Love**
  - a. **Compassion ~ Non-Judgmental Compassionate regard for Self, Others & the World**
  - b. **Self-Love ~ Treat Yourself the way you would a Child or your Best Friend**
  - c. **Love of Others ~ Your Presence in the Present Moment, Deep Listening & Unconditionally Loving Speech**
  - d. **Love of the World ~ Be of Service to the Collective, Live Gently & Simply**
- **Step 2 – Integrating the Feminine and the Masculine**
  - a. **Feminine**
    - i. **Transition from Doing to Being**

ii. **Surrender & Vulnerability ~ Connecting with Emotions & Needs**

iii. **Self-Trust ~ Embracing the Intuition**

b. **Masculine**

   i. **Setting Boundaries & Limits ~ Saying No**

   ii. **Self-Respect ~ Transition from being "Too Nice" to "Healthy Assertiveness"**

   iii. **Claiming your Courage & Wisdom ~ Own It**

- **Step 3 – Making the Unconscious Conscious**

   a. **Journaling**

   b. **Meditation**

   c. **Dream Analysis**

   d. **Expressive Arts (Drawing, Painting, Dancing, Active Imagination, etc.)**

CONCLUSION

This is the perfect time for us to shape our own destiny. The advances we make now will set a new standard for women everywhere. There are many possibilities in life beyond what we may presently think or experience. We now have opportunities never available to women before. It is time to connect with other women, to improve life for all women. This will, in turn, improve life for men. When women are fulfilled, satisfied and happy, they will be wonderful partners, wonderful people to work with and to live with. And men will feel infinitely more comfortable with equals! (Hay, 1997, pp. 155-156)

The 21st century is a time of change where women are experiencing a crisis of the soul. Empowerment and happiness are important and different for every woman. The participants interviewed spoke of being called to greater fulfillment in their lives while recognizing that conscious active responsibility would be necessary to satisfy those needs. In many cases, it remained unknown whether the participants would decide to act upon the insights and impulses or not. Our findings suggest that fear-based survival mode are keeping women who outwardly seem empowered from an inner feeling of empowerment, and thus from happiness. Society needs to attend to these findings that are so critical to health (psychologically/physically) and reflect deeply on how to help women find the courage to move forward.

The participants are among those Western women who are a part of the vanguards who infiltrated the male dominated workforce and advanced toward significant professional empowerment. It is of great importance that we pay attention to such women's interpretation of their experiences. It is clear that women's emotional, mental, physical and spiritual health would be improved through access to specific therapeutic modalities. These should be based on these three steps: unconditional love, integration of the feminine and the masculine, and making the unconscious conscious, which is designed to access the individual's inner sage and as yet unrealized potentialities. A healthy society does rely on women rising, owning their experience, balancing their priorities, and having access to steps for health. We hope that this research will make individuals aware of the challenges women confront, and their need to move forward toward empowerment and happiness, thereby healing the world.

REFERENCES

Adamczyk, A. (2014, April 21). *Experts say women must learn to negotiate their salaries in college to close the gender wage gap.* Retrieved from http://college.usatoday.com

Adamczyk, A. (2015, November 4th). *These are the companies with the best parental leave policies.* Retrieved from http://time.com/money/4098469/paid-parental-leave-google-amazon-apple-facebook/

Amen, D. (2013). *Unleashing the power of the feminine brain.* New York, NY: Random House.

Becker, H. (2007). *Unconditional love: An unlimited way of being.* Cumberland, MD: White Fire.

Berceo, G. (1997). *Miracles of Our Lady.* Lexington, KY: University Press of Kentucky.

Bianchi, S., Robinson, S., & Milkie, M. (2006). *Changing rhythms of American family life.* New York, NY: Russell Sage Foundation.

Campbell, J. (1988). *The power of myth.* New York, NY: Doubleday.

Campbell, J. (1990). *The hero's journey.* Novato, CA: New World Library.

Campbell, J. (2004). *Pathways to bliss.* Novato, CA: New World Library.

Campbell, J. (2013). *Goddesses: Mysteries of the feminine divine. In collected works of Joseph Campbell.* Novato, CA: New World Library.

Cavalli, T. (2002). *Alchemical psychology.* New York, NY: Putnam Books.

Creswell, J. W. (1998). *Qualitative inquiry and research design: Choosing among five traditions.* Thousand Oaks, CA: Sage.

Crittenden, A. (2010). *The price of motherhood: why the most important job in the world is still the least valued.* London, England: Picador.

Dishman, L. (2015, November 3rd). *What's missing from amazon's new parental leave policy.* Retrieved from http://m.fastcompany.com/3053093/second-shift/whats-missing-from-amazons-new-parental-leave-policy

Downing, C. (1981/2007). *The goddess: mythological images of the feminine.* Spring Valley, NY: Crossroad Pub

Downing, C. (1995/2004). *The luxury of afterwards: The Christine Downing lectures at San Diego State University (1995-2004).* Bloomington, IN: iUniverse

Eisler, R. (1987). *The chalice and the blade.* New York, NY: Harper & Row.

Evans, S., & Avis, J. (1999). *The women who broke all the rules.* Naperville, IL: Sourcebooks.

Fitzpatrick, L. (2009, Oct 14). The state of the American woman. *Time*, 29.

Flinn, S. (2000). *Speaking of Hillary: A reader's guide to the most controversial woman in America.* Ashland, OR: White Cloud Press.

Gadamer, H. (1983). Hermeneutics as practical philosophy. In F. G. Lawrence (Trans.), *Reason in the age of science* (pp. 88-138). Cambridge, MA: The MIT Press. (Original work published 1981)

Gadamer, H. G. (1988). Truth and method (2nd ed.) New York, NY: Continuum. (Original work published 1960)

Gadon, E. (1989). *The once and future goddess.* New York, NY: Harper & Row.

Gandhi, M. (1962). *The essential Gandhi.* New York, NY: Random House.

Gibbs, N. (2009, October 14). The state of the American woman. *Time*, 25-33.

Gilbert, D. (2006). *Stumbling on happiness.* New York, NY: Random House.

Gilbert, E. (2006). *Eat pray love.* New York, NY: Penguin Books.

Gore, A. (2010). *Bluebird women and the new psychology of happiness.* New York, NY: Farrar, Straus and Giroux.

Graham, L. (1997). *Goddesses in art.* New York, NY: Abbeville Press.

Hail, R. (2000). *The Cherokee sacred calendar.* Rochester, VT: Destiny Books.

Harding, M. E. (1970). *The way of all women.* Boston, MA: Shambhala.

Harvey, A. (1998). *Son of man.* New York, NY: Putnam Books.

Hay, L. (1997). *Empowering woman.* Carlsbad, CA: Hay House.

Hodgkinson, G. P. (2008). Intuition: A fundamental bridging construct in the behavioural sciences. *British Journal of Psychology, 99,* 1-27.

Husserl, E. (1980). *Phenomenology and the foundations of the sciences.* Boston, MA: Martinus Hijhoff. (Original work published 1952)

Ihde, D. (1983). *Interpreting hermeneutics: Origins, developments, prospects. In Existential technics* (pp. 137-157). Albany: State University of New York Press.

Jacobi, J. (1973). *The psychology of C. G. Jung.* London, England: Yale University Press. (Original work published 1969)

Johnson, R. (1990). *Femininity lost and regained.* New York, NY: Harper.

Jung, C. G. (1971). *Psychological types. In The collected works of C. G. Jung* (Vol. 6). London, England: Routledge. (Original work published 1921)

Jung, C. G. (1972). Two essays on analytical psychology. In H. Read, M. Fordham, G. Adler, & W. McGuire (Eds.), *The collected works of C. G. Jung* (R. F. C. Hull, Trans.) (2nd ed., Vol. 7). Princeton, NJ: Princeton University Press. (Original works published 1943 & 1928)

Jung, C. G. (1980). *Analytical psychology in a changing world.* London, England: Routledge. (Original work published 1959)

Jung, C. G. (1982). *Aspects of the masculine and aspects of the feminine.* New York, NY: Princeton University Press.

Jung, E. (1987). *Animus and anima.* Dallas, TX: Spring. (Original work published 1957)

Knapp, B. (1987). *Women in twentieth-century literature: A Jungian view.* University Park, PA: Pennsylvania State University Press.

Kristof, N., & WuDunn, S. (2009). *Half the sky: Turning oppression into opportunity for women worldwide.* New York, NY: Random House.

Kristof, N., & WuDunn, S. (2009, August 17). Saving the world's women: The women's crusade. *The New York Times.*

Kurtz, E., & Ketcham, K. (1993). *The spirituality of imperfection: Storytelling and the search for meaning.* New York, NY: Random House.

Labov, W. (1997). Narrative analysis. *The Journal of Narrative and Life History, 7*(1-4), 395-415

Lerner, G. (1987). *The creation of patriarchy (Women and history).* New York, NY: Oxford University Press.

Maslow, A. (2011). *Toward a psychology of being.* Blacksburg, VA: Wilder.

Morris, W. (1986). Empowerment. In *The New Webster's Dictionary* (p. 59). London, England: T. Nelson.

Morris, W. (1986). Happiness. In *The New Webster's Dictionary* (p. 81). London, England: T. Nelson.

Mundy, L. (2012). *The richer sex.* New York, NY: Simon & Schuster.

Myers, D. D. (2008). *Why women should rule the world.* New York, NY: HarperCollins.

Newman, M., & Berkowitz, B. (1971). *How to be your own best friend.* New York, NY: Random House.

Palmer, R. (1969). *Hermeneutics.* Evanston, IL: Northwestern University Press.

Parrish-Harra, C. (1988). *The aquarian rosary: Reviving the art of mantra yoga.* Tahlequah, OK: Sparrow Hawk Press.

Pipher, M. (1994). *Reviving Ophelia.* New York, NY: Berkeley.

REFERENCES

Polkinghorne, D. (1983). *Methodology for the human sciences: Systems of inquiry.* Albany: State University of New York Press.

Poulsen, L. (2013). *5 traits of a good account manager.* Retrieved from http://www.businessbee.com

Public and Private. (2014, June 9). Retrieved from ABCnews.go.com/WNT/video/diane-sawyers-exclusive-interview-hillary-clinton-24064003

Rahula, W. (1959). *What the Buddha taught.* New York, NY: Grove Press.

Ravikant, K. (2012). *Love yourself like your life depends on it.* Retrieved from www.CreateSpace.com

Raye, R. (2006). *Have the relationship you want.* Retrieved from Lulu.com

Riddle, K. (2013). *Channel your goddess energy.* New York, NY: CICO Books.

Sapolsky, R. (2004). *Why zebras don't get ulcers.* New York, NY: Holt.

Sanford, J. (1980). *The invisible partners.* New York, NY: Paulist Press.

Schnarch, D. (1997). *Passionate marriage: Sex, love, and intimacy in emotionally committed relationships.* New York, NY: Norton.

Shimoff, M. (2010). *Love for no reason.* New York, NY: Free Press/Simon & Schuster.

Shlain, L. (2003). *Sex, time, and power: How women's sexuality shaped human evolution.* New York, NY: Penguin.

Spencer, A. (1908). *Woman's share in social culture.* Princeton, NJ: M. Kennerley.

Thoele, S. (1991). *The courage to be yourself.* Berkeley, CA: Conari Press. (Original work published 1988)

UNWomen.org. (2015, December). *Facts and figures: leadership and political participation.* Retrieved from http://www.unwomen.org/en/what-we-do/leadership-and-political-participation/facts-and-figures

Williams, J. (2010). *Reshaping the work-family debate: Why men and class matter.* London, England: Harvard University Press.

TRACY ULOMA COOPER

Tracy Cooper is a Ph.D. in Clinical Psychology, specializing in integrative therapy and personal empowerment. At the University of California, Berkeley she was a psychotherapist within the Psychological Services department. Presently, she is a psychotherapist offering comprehensive care to patients with chronic medical conditions and serious mental illness. As a community activist, she is involved with several nonprofit organizations. She is the founder of The Uloma Foundation, she serves as a board member for Arts for All, and manages a mental health program at Interfaith Community Services. Tracy Cooper is an academic and literary author. She contributed to the book *What Women Want: A Book for Men* and she is the author of the children's book series *Sophie Starchild*.

CPSIA information can be obtained
at www.ICGtesting.com
Printed in the USA
FFOW04n0711010318
45375490-46074FF